We will gather buds and locust-blossoms, leaves and honeysuckle
To wreathe around our foreheads, riding into Used-to-Be

Memorial Edition

The Complete Works of
James Whitcomb Riley

IN TEN VOLUMES

*Including Poems and Prose Sketches, many
of which have not heretofore been published; an authentic Biography, an
elaborate Index and numerous
Illustrations from Paintings
by Howard Chandler Christy
and Ethel Franklin Betts*

VOLUME III

*BOBBS-MERRILL
EDITION*

PUBLISHED BY

P. F. COLLIER & SON COMPANY

NEW YORK

CONTENTS

CONTENTS

CONTENTS

CONTENTS

CONTENTS

The Complete Works
of James Whitcomb Riley

THE PASSING OF A HEART

O TOUCH me with your hands—
                    For pity's sake!
My brow throbs ever on with such an ache
As only your cool touch may take away;
And so, I pray
                    You, touch me with your hands!

Touch—touch me with your hands.—
                    Smooth back the hair
You once caressed, and kissed, and called so fair
That I did dream its gold would wear alway,
And lo, to-day—
                    O touch me with your hands!

Just touch me with your hands,
                    And let them press
My weary eyelids with the old caress,
And lull me till I sleep.   Then go your way,
That Death may say:
                    He touched her with his hands.

AN OLD-TIMER

HERE where the wayward stream
        Is restful as a dream,
    And where the banks o'erlook
A pool from out whose deeps
My pleased face upward peeps,
        I cast my hook.

Silence and sunshine blent!—
A Sabbath-like content
    Of wood and wave;—a free-
Hand landscape grandly wrought
Of Summer's brightest thought
        And mastery.—

For here form, light and shade,
And color—all are laid
    With skill so rarely fine,
The eye may even see
The ripple tremblingly
        Lip at the line.

I mark the dragon-fly
Flit waveringly by
    In ever-veering flight,

Till, in a hush profound,
I see him eddy round
    The "cork," and—'light!

Ho! with the boy's faith then
Brimming my heart again,
  And knowing, soon or late,
The "nibble" yet shall roll
Its thrills along the pole,
    I—breathless—wait.

ERE I WENT MAD

ERE I went mad—
    O you may never guess what dreams I had!
Such hosts of happy things did come to me.
One time, it seemed, I knelt at some one's knee,
My wee lips threaded with a strand of prayer,
With kinks of kisses in it here and there
To stay and tangle it the while I knit
A mother's long-forgotten name in it.
Be sure, I dreamed it all, but I was glad
—Ere I went mad!

Ere I went mad,
I dreamed there came to me a fair-faced lad,
Who led me by the wrist where blossoms grew
In grassy lands, and where the skies were blue
As his own eyes. And he did lisp and sing,
And weave me wreaths where I sat marveling
What little prince it was that crowned me queen
And caught my face so cunningly between
His dimple-dinted hands, and kept me glad
—Ere I went mad!

576

Ere I went mad,
Not even winter weather made me sad·
I dreamed, indeed, the skies were ne'er so dull
That *his* smile might not make them beautiful.
And now, it seemed, he had grown O so fair
And straight and strong that, when he smoothed
     my hair,
I felt as any lily with drooped head
That leans, in fields of grain unharvested,
By some lithe stalk of barley—pure and glad
—Ere I went mad!

Ere I went mad,
The last of all the happy dreams I had
Was of a peerless king—a conqueror—
Who crowned me with a kiss, and throned me for
One hour! Ah, God of Mercy! what a dream
To tincture life with! Yet I made no scream
As I awakened—with these eyes you see,
That may not smile till love comes back to me,
And lulls me back to those old dreams I had
—Ere I went mad!

OH, HER BEAUTY

OH, her beauty was such that it dazzled my
    eyes
Like a dreamer's, who, gazing in day-dying skies,
Sees the snow of the clouds and the gold of the sun
And the blue of the heavens all blended in one
Indescribable luster of glorious light,
Swooning into the moon of a midsummer night.

Oh, her beauty was such that I fancied her hair
Was a cloud of the tempest, tied up with a glare
Of pale purple lightning, that darted and ran
Through the coils like the blood in the veins of a
    man:
And from dark silken billows that girdled her
    free,
Her shoulder welled up like the moon from the sea.

Oh, her beauty was such, as I knelt, with the tips
Of the fingers uplifted she snatched from my lips,
And saw the white flood of her wrath as it dashed
O'er the features, that one moment later had flashed
From my vision forever, I raised not a knee
Till I had thanked God for so rescuing me.

THE SUMMER-TIME

O THE Summer-time to-day
　　Makes my words
Jes' flip up and fly away
　　Like the birds!
　　　　—'Tain't no use to try to sing,
　　　　With yer language on the wing,
　　　　Jes' too glad fer anything
　　　　　　But to stray
　　　　　　　Where it may
Thue the sunny summer weather of the day!

　　Lordy! what a Summer-time
　　　　Fer to sing!
　　But my words flops out o' rhyme,
　　　　And they wing
　　　　　　Furder yit beyent the view
　　　　　　Than the swallers ever flew,
　　　　　　Er a mortal wanted to—
　　　　　　　'Less his eye
　　　　　　　　Struck the sky
Ez he kind o' sort o' thought he'd like to fly!

Ef I *could* sing—sweet and low—
  And my tongue
Could *twitter,* don't you know,—
   Ez I sung
    Of the Summer-time, 'y Jings!
    All the words and birds and things
    That kin warble, and hes wings,
     Would jes' swear
     And declare
That they never heerd sich singin' anywhere!

SONG OF PARTING

SAY farewell, and let me go:
  Shatter every vow!
All the future can bestow
  Will be welcome now!
    And if this fair hand I touch
    I have worshiped overmuch,
    It was my mistake—and so,
    Say farewell, and let me go.

Say farewell, and let me go:
  Murmur no regret,
Stay your tear-drops ere they flow—
  Do not waste them yet!
    They might pour as pours the rain,
    And not wash away the pain:—
    I have tried them and I know.—
    Say farewell, and let me go.

Say farewell, and let me go:
  Think me not untrue—
True as truth is, even so
  I am true to you!
    If the ghost of love may stay
    Where my fond heart dies to-day,
    I am with you alway—so,
    Say farewell, and let me go.

THE WANDERING JEW

THE stars are failing, and the sky
  Is like a field of faded flowers
The winds on weary wings go by;
  The moon hides, and the tempest lowers;
    And still through every clime and age
    I wander on a pilgrimage
    That all men know an idle quest,
    For that the goal I seek is—REST!

I hear the voice of summer streams,
  And, following, I find the brink
Of cooling springs, with childish dreams
  Returning as I bend to drink—
    But suddenly, with startled eyes,
    My face looks on its grim disguise
    Of long gray beard; and so, distressed,
    I hasten on, nor taste of rest.

I came upon a merry group
  Of children in the dusky wood,
Who answer back the owlet's whoop,
  That laughs as it had understood;
    And I would pause a little space,
    But that each happy blossom-face
    Is like to one *His* hands have blessed
    Who sent me forth in search of rest.

Sometimes I fain would stay my feet
　　In shady lanes, where huddled kine
Couch in the grasses cool and sweet,
　　　And lift their patient eyes to mine;
　　　　　But I, for thoughts that ever then
　　　　　Go back to Bethlehem again,
　　　　　Must needs fare on my weary quest,
　　　　　And weep for very need of rest.

Is there no end?   I plead in vain:
　　Lost worlds nor living answer me.
Since Pontius Pilate's awful reign
　　Have I not passed eternity?
　　　　　Have I not drunk the fetid breath
　　　　　Of every fevered phase of death,
　　　　　And come unscathed through every pest
　　　　　And scourge and plague that promised
　　　　　　　rest?

Have I not seen the stars go out
　　That shed their light o'er Galilee,
And mighty kingdoms tossed about
　　And crumbled clod-like in the sea?
　　　　　Dead ashes of dead ages blow
　　　　　And cover me like drifting snow,
　　　　　And time laughs on as 'twere a jest
　　　　　That I have any need of rest.

THE USED-TO-BE

BEYOND the purple, hazy trees
  Of summer's utmost boundaries;
Beyond the sands—beyond the seas—
Beyond the range of eyes iike these,
  And only in the reach of the
  Enraptured gaze of Memory,
    There lies a land, long lost to me,—
      The land of Used-to-be!

A land enchanted—such as swung
In golden seas when sirens clung
Along their dripping brinks, and sung
To Jason in that mystic tongue
  That dazed men with its melody—
  O such a land, with such a sea
  Kissing its shores eternally,
    Is the fair Used-to-be.

A land where music ever girds
The air with belts of singing-birds,
And sows all sounds with such sweet
      words,

That even in the low of herds
  A meaning lives so sweet to me,
  Lost laughter ripples limpidly
  From lips brimmed over with the glee
    Of rare old Used-to-be.

Lost laughter, and the whistled tunes
Of boyhood's mouth of crescent runes,
That rounded, through long afternoons,
To serenading plenilunes—
  When starlight fell so mistily
  That, peering up from bended knee,
  I dreamed 'twas bridal drapery
    Snowed over Used-to-be.

O land of love and dreamy thoughts,
And shining fields, and shady spots
Of coolest, greenest grassy plots,
Embossed with wild forget-me-nots!—
  And all ye blooms that longingly
  Lift your fair faces up to me
  Out of the past, I kiss in ye
    The lips of Used-to-be.

AT UTTER LOAF

I

AN afternoon as ripe with heat
As might the golden pippin be
With mellowness if at my feet
It dropped now from the apple-tree
My hammock swings in lazily.

II

The boughs about me spread a shade
That shields me from the sun, but weaves
With breezy shuttles through the leaves
Blue rifts of skies, to gleam and fade
Upon the eyes that only see
Just of themselves, all drowsily.

III

Above me drifts the fallen skein
Of some tired spider, looped and blown,
As fragile as a strand of rain,
Across the air, and upward thrown
By breaths of hay-fields newly mown—
So glimmering it is and fine,
I doubt these drowsy eyes of mine.

IV

Far-off and faint as voices pent
    In mines, and heard from underground,
Come murmurs as of discontent,
    And clamorings of sullen sound
The city sends me, as, I guess,
To vex me, though they do but bless
Me in my drowsy fastnesses.

V

I have no care. I only know
    My hammock hides and holds me here
    In lands of shade a prisoner:
While lazily the breezes blow
    Light leaves of sunshine over me,
And back and forth and to and fro
    I swing, enwrapped in some hushed glee,
    Smiling at all things drowsily.

MY OLD FRIEND

YOU'VE a manner all so mellow,
    My old friend,
That it cheers and warms a fellow,
    My old friend,
Just to meet and greet you, and
Feel the pressure of a hand
That one may understand,
    My old friend.

Though dimmed in youthful splendor,
    My old friend,
Your smiles are still as tender,
    My old friend,
And your eyes as true a blue
As your childhood ever knew,
And your laugh as merry, too,
    My old friend.

For though your hair is faded,
    My old friend,
And your step a trifle jaded,
    My old friend,

Old Time, with all his lures
In the trophies he secures,
Leaves young that heart of yours,
        My old friend.

And so it is you cheer me,
        My old friend,
For to know you and be near you,
        My old friend,
Makes my hopes of clearer light,
And my faith of surer sight,
And my soul a purer white,
        My old friend.

KISSING THE ROD

O HEART of mine, we shouldn't
        Worry so!
What we've missed of calm we couldn't
        Have, you know!
What we've met of stormy pain,
And of sorrow's driving rain,
We can better meet again,
        If it blow!

We have erred in that dark hour
        We have known,
When our tears fell with the shower,
        All alone!—
Were not shine and shower blent
As the gracious Master meant?—
Let us temper our content
        With His own.

For, we know, not every morrow
        Can be sad;
So, forgetting all the sorrow
        We have had,
Let us fold away our fears,
And put by our foolish tears,
And through all the coming years
        Just be glad.

THE RIVAL

I SO loved once, when Death came by I hid
    Away my face,
And all my sweetheart's tresses she undid
    To make my hiding-place.

The dread shade passed me thus unheeding; and
    I turned me then
To calm my love—kiss down her shielding hand
    And comfort her again.

And lo! she answered not: And she did sit
    All fixedly,
With her fair face and the sweet smile of it,
    In love with Death, not me.

THE LIGHT OF LOVE

SONG

THE clouds have deepened o'er the night
   Till, through the dark profound,
The moon is but a stain of light,
   And all the stars are drowned;
And all the stars are drowned, my love,
   And all the skies are drear;
But what care we for light above,
   If light of love is here?

The wind is like a wounded thing
   That beats about the gloom
With baffled breast and drooping wing,
   And wail of deepest doom;
And wail of deepest doom, my love;
   But what have we to fear
From night, or rain, or winds above,
   With love and laughter here?

LET SOMETHING GOOD BE SAID

WHEN over the fair fame of friend or foe
    The shadow of disgrace shall fall, instead
Of words of blame, or proof of thus and so,
    Let something good be said.

Forget not that no fellow-being yet
    May fall so low but love may lift his head:
Even the cheek of shame with tears is wet,
    If something good be said.

No generous heart may vainly turn aside
    In ways of sympathy; no soul so dead
But may awaken strong and glorified,
    If something good be said.

And so I charge ye, by the thorny crown,
    And by the cross on which the Saviour bled,
And by your own soul's hope of fair renown,
    Let something good be said!

THE OLD HAND-ORGAN

HARSH-VOICED it was, and shrill and high,
　With hesitating stops and stutters,
As though the vagrant melody,
　　Playing so long about the gutters,
　　Had been infected with some low
　　Malignant type of vertigo.

A stark-eyed man that stared the sun
　　Square in the face, and without winking;
His soldier cap pushed back, and one
　　Scarred hand that grasped the crank,
　　　　unshrinking—
　　But from the jingling discord made
　　By shamefaced pennies as he played.

HOME AT NIGHT

WHEN chirping crickets fainter cry,
  And pale stars blossom in the sky,
And twilight's gloom has dimmed the bloom
And blurred the butterfly:

When locust-blossoms fleck the walk,
And up the tiger-lily stalk
The glowworm crawls and clings and falls
And glimmers down the garden-walls:

When buzzing things, with double wings
Of crisp and raspish flutterings,
Go whizzing by so very nigh
One thinks of fangs and stings:—

O then, within, is stilled the din
Of crib she rocks the baby in,
And heart and gate and latch's weight
Are lifted—and the lips of Kate.

A DREAM OF INSPIRATION

TO loll back, in a misty hammock, swung
　From tip to tip of a slim crescent moon
That gems some royal-purple night of June—
To dream of songs that never have been sung
Since the first stars were stilled and God was young
　And Heaven as lonesome as a lonesome tune:
　To lie thus, lost to earth, with lids aswoon;
By curious, cool winds back and forward flung,
　With fluttering hair, blurred eyes, and utter ease
Adrift like lazy blood through every vein;
　And then,—the pulse of unvoiced melodies
Timing the raptured sense to some refrain
　That knows nor words, nor rhymes, nor
　　euphonies,
　Save Fancy's hinted chime of unknown seas.

THE PIPER'S SON

IN olden days there dwelt a piper's son,
  Hight Thomas, who, belike from indigence,
  Or utter lack of virtuous preference
Of honorable means of thrift, did, one
Weak hour of temptation—(weaker none!)—
  Put by ye promptings of his better sense,
  And rashly gat him o'er a neighbor's fence
Wherein ye corner was a paling run
About a goodly pig; and thence he lured,
  All surreptitiously, ye hapless beast,
And had it slaughtered, salted down, and cured—
  Yea, even tricked and garnished for ye feast,
Ere yet ye red-eyed Law had him immured,
  And round and soundly justice-of-ye-peaced.

HIS LAST PICTURE

THE skies have grown troubled and dreary;
  The clouds gather fold upon fold;
The hand of the painter is weary
  And the pencil has dropped from its hold:
The easel still leans in the grasses,
  And the palette beside on the lawn,
But the rain o'er the sketch as it passes
  Weeps low—for the artist is gone.

The flowers whose fairy-like features
  Smiled up in his own as he wrought,
And the leaves and the ferns were his teachers,
  And the tints of the sun what they taught;
The low-swinging vines, and the mosses—
  The shadow-filled boughs of the trees,
And the blossomy spray as it tosses
  The song of the bird to the breeze.

The silent white laugh of the lily
  He learned; and the smile of the rose
Glowed back on his spirit until he
  Had mastered the blush as it glows;

And his pencil has touched and caressed them,
  And kissed them, through breaths of perfume,
To the canvas that yet shall have blessed them
  With years of unwithering bloom.

Then come!—Leave his palette and brushes
  And easel there, just as his hand
Has left them, ere through the dark hushes
  Of death, to the shadowy land,
He wended his way, happy-hearted
  As when, in his youth, his rapt eyes
Swept the pathway of Fame where it started,
  To where it wound into the skies.

A VARIATION

I AM tired of this!
Nothing else but loving!
Nothing else but kiss and kiss,
Coo, and turtle-doving!
Can't you change the order some?
Hate me just a little—come!

Lay aside your "dears,"
"Darlings," "kings," and "princes!"
Call me knave, and dry your tears—
Nothing in me winces,—
Call me something low and base—
Something that will suit the case!

Wish I had your eyes
And their drooping lashes!
I would dry their teary lies
Up with lightning-flashes—
Make your sobbing lips unsheathe
All the glitter of your teeth!

Can't you lift one word—
With some pang of laughter—
Louder than the drowsy bird

Crooning 'neath the rafter?
  Just one bitter word, to shriek
  Madly at me as I speak!

How I hate the fair
  Beauty of your forehead!
How I hate your fragrant hair!
  How I hate the torrid
    Touches of your splendid lips,
    And the kiss that drips and drips!

Ah, you pale at last!
  And your face is lifted
Like a white sail to the blast,
  And your hands are shifted
    Into fists: and, towering thus,
    You are simply glorious!

Now before me looms
  Something more than human;
Something more than beauty blooms
  In the wrath of Woman—
    Something to bow down before
    Reverently and adore.

THERE IS A NEED

THERE is a need for every ache or pain
   That falls unto our lot. No heart may bleed
That resignation may not heal again
         And teach us—there's a need.

There is a need for every tear that drips
   Adown the face of sorrow. None may heed,
But weeping washes whiter on the lips
         Our prayers—and there's a need.

There is a need for weariness and dearth
   Of all that brings delight. At topmost speed
Of pleasure sobs may break amid our mirth
         Unheard—and there's a need.

There is a need for all the growing load
   Of agony we bear as years succeed;
For lo, the Master's footprints in the road
         Before us—There's a need.

TO A SKULL

TURN your face this way;
    I'm not weary of it—
Every hour of every day
    More and more I love it—
Grinning in that jolly guise
Of bare bones and empty eyes!

Was this hollow dome,
    Where I tap my finger,
Once the spirit's narrow home—
    Where you loved to linger,
Hiding, as to-day are we,
From the selfsame destiny?

O'er and o'er again
    Have I put the query—
Was existence so in vain
    That you look so cheery?—
Death of such a benefit
That you smile, possessing it?

Did your throbbing brow
    Tire of all the flutter
Of such fancyings as now

You, at last, may utter
In that grin so grimly bland
Only death can understand?

Has the shallow glee
   Of old dreams of pleasure
Left you ever wholly free
   To float out, at leisure,
O'er the shoreless, trackless trance
Of unsounded circumstance?

Only this I read
   In your changeless features,—
You, at least, have gained a meed
   Held from living creatures:
You have naught to ask.—Beside,
You do grin so satisfied!

THE VOICES

DOWN in the night I hear them:
  The Voices—unknown—unguessed,—
That whisper, and lisp, and murmur,
  And will not let me rest.—

Voices that seem to question,
  In unknown words, of me,
Of fabulous ventures, and hopes and dreams
  Of this and the World to be.

Voices of mirth and music,
  As in sumptuous homes; and sounds
Of mourning, as of gathering friends
  In country burial-grounds.

Cadence of maiden voices—
  Their lovers' blent with these;
And of little children singing,
  As under orchard trees.

And often, up from the chaos
  Of my deepest dreams, I hear
Sounds of their phantom laughter
  Filling the atmosphere:

They call to me from the darkness;
  They cry to me from the gloom,
Till I start sometimes from my pillow
  And peer through the haunted room;

When the face of the moon at the window
  Wears a pallor like my own,
And seems to be listening with me
  To the low, mysterious tone,—

The low, mysterious clamor
  Of voices that seem to be
Striving in vain to whisper
  Of secret things to me;—

Of a something dread to be warned of;
  Of a rapture yet withheld;
Or hints of the marvelous beauty
  Of songs unsyllabled.

But ever and ever the meaning
  Falters and fails and dies,
And only the silence quavers
  With the sorrow of my sighs.

And I answer:—O Voices, ye may not
  Make me to understand
Till my own voice, mingling with you,
  Laughs in the Shadow-land.

MY HENRY

HE'S jes' a great, big, awk'ard, hulkin'
    Feller,—humped, and sort o' sulkin'-
Like, and ruther still-appearin'—
Kind-as-ef he wuzn't keerin'
      Whether school helt out er not—
      That's my Henry, to a dot!

Allus kind o' liked him—whether
Childern, er growed-up together!
Fifteen year' ago and better,
'Fore he ever knowed a letter,
      Run acrosst the little fool
      In my Primer-class at school.

When the Teacher wuzn't lookin',
He'd be th'owin' wads; er crookin'
Pins; er sprinklin' pepper, more'n
Likely, on the stove; er borin'
      Gimlet-holes up thue his desk—
      Nothin' *that* boy wouldn't resk!

But, somehow, as I was goin'
On to say, he seemed so knowin',
Other ways, and cute and cunnin'—

Allus wuz a notion runnin'
    Thue my giddy, fool-head he
    Jes' had be'n cut out fer me!

Don't go much on *prophesyin'*,
But last night whilse I wuz fryin'
Supper, with that man a-pitchin'
Little Marthy round the kitchen,
    Think-says-I, "Them baby's eyes
    Is my Henry's, jes' p'cise!"

LOVE'S AS BROAD AS LONG

LOOKY here!—you fellers—you
   Poets I'm a-talkin' to,—
Allus rhymin', right er wrong,
'Bout your "little" love, and "long"—
'Pears to me 'at nary one
Of you fellers gits much fun
Out o' lovin'—tryin' to fit
Out some fool-receet fer it!—
     Love's as broad as long!

Now, I 'low 'at love's a thing
You cain't jes' set down and sing
Out your order fer, and say
You'll hev yourn a certain way;
And how "long" a slice you'll take,
Er how short—'cause love don't make
No distinctions, and you'll find,
When it comes, it's all one kind—
     Jes' as broad as long!

Fust, one of you'll p'tend
"Love's no idle song," and send
Up his voice in jes' the song
He's th'owed up on—"Love me long!"

Now, they hain't no womern needs
No sich talk as that!—er heeds
Sich advice as would infer
You hed any doubts o' her!
    Love's as broad as long.

Ner I don't see any use,
Er occasion, er excuse
Fer some other chap to say,
In his passioneter way,
"Love me madly, as of yore!"—
'Cause I've seed sich love afore,
'At got fellers down, and jes'
Wooled 'em round till they confessed
    Love was broad as long.

No; I'll tell you: You jes' let
Love alone, and you kin bet,
When the time comes, Love'll be
Right on hands as punctchully
As he was the day Eve sot
Waitin', in the gyarden-spot,
Fer ole Adam jes' to go
On ahead and tell her so!
    Love's as broad as long!

LOCKERBIE STREET

SUCH a dear little street it is, nestled away
From the noise of the city and heat of the day,
In cool shady coverts of whispering trees,
With their leaves lifted up to shake hands with the
    breeze
Which in all its wide wanderings never may meet
With a resting-place fairer than Lockerbie Street!

There is such a relief, from the clangor and din
Of the heart of the town, to go loitering in
Through the dim, narrow walks, with the sheltering
    shade
Of the trees waving over the long promenade,
And littering lightly the ways of our feet
With the gold of the sunshine of Lockerbie Street.

And the nights that come down the dark pathways
    of dusk,
With the stars in their tresses, and odors of musk
In their moon-woven raiments, bespangled with
    dews,
And looped up with lilies for lovers to use

In the songs that they sing to the tinkle and beat
Of their sweet serenadings through Lockerbie
    Street.

O my Lockerbie Street! You are fair to be seen—
Be it noon of the day, or the rare and serene
Afternoon of the night—you are one to my heart,
And I love you above all the phrases of art,
For no language could frame and no lips could
    repeat
My rhyme-haunted raptures of Lockerbie Street.

THE OLD, OLD WISH

LAST night, in some lost mood of meditation,
    The while my dreamy vision ranged the far
Unfathomable arches of creation,
        I saw a falling star:

And as my eyes swept round the path it embered
    With the swift-dying glory of its glow,
With sudden intuition I remembered
        A wish of long ago—

A wish that, were it made—so ran the fancy
    Of credulous young lover and of lass—
As fell a star, by some strange necromancy,
        Would surely come to pass.

And, of itself, the wish, reiterated
    A thousand times in youth, flashed o'er my
        brain,
And, like the star, as soon obliterated,
        Dropped into night again.

For my old heart had wished for the unending
   Devotion of a little maid of nine—
And that the girl-heart, with the woman's
     blending,
       Might be forever mine.

And so it was, with eyelids raised, and weighty
   With ripest clusterings of sorrow's dew,
I cried aloud through Heaven: "O little Katie!
      When will my wish come true?"

A LIFE-LESSON

THERE! little girl; don't cry!
    They have broken your doll, I know;
      And your tea-set blue,
      And your play-house, too,
    Are things of the long ago;
      But childish troubles will soon pass by.—
        There! little girl; don't cry!

There! little girl; don't cry!
    They have broken your slate, I know;
      And the glad, wild ways
      Of your schoolgirl days
    Are things of the long ago;
      But life and love will soon come by.—
        There! little girl; don't cry!

There! little girl; don't cry!
    They have broken your heart, I know;
      And the rainbow gleams
      Of your youthful dreams
    Are things of the long ago;
      But Heaven holds all for which you sigh.—
        There! little girl; don't cry!

A WATER-COLOR

LOW hidden in among the forest trees
    An artist's tilted easel, ankle-deep
In tousled ferns and mosses, and in these
    A fluffy water-spaniel, half asleep
        Beside a sketch-book and a fallen hat—
        A little wicker flask tossed into that.

A sense of utter carelessness and grace
    Of pure abandon in the slumb'rous scene,—
As if the June, all hoydenish of face,
    Had romped herself to sleep there on the
                green,
        And brink and sagging bridge and sliding
            stream
        Were just romantic parcels of her dream.

UNKNOWN FRIENDS

O FRIENDS of mine, whose kindly words come
to me
Voiced only in lost lisps of ink and pen,
If I had power to tell the good you do me,
And how the blood you warm goes laughing through
me,
My tongue would babble baby-talk again.

And I would toddle round the world to meet you—
Fall at your feet, and clamber to your knees
And with glad, happy hands would reach and greet
you,
And twine my arms about you, and entreat you
For leave to weave a thousand rhymes like
these—

A thousand rhymes enwrought of nought but
presses
Of cherry-lip and apple-cheek and chin,
And pats of honeyed palms, and rare caresses,
And all the sweets of which as Fancy guesses
She folds away her wings and swoons therein.

THE SONG OF YESTERDAY

I

BUT yesterday
I looked away
O'er happy lands, where sunshine lay
    In golden blots,
    Inlaid with spots
Of shade and wild forget-me-nots.

    My head was fair
    With flaxen hair,
And fragrant breezes, faint and rare,
    And, warm with drouth
    From out the south,
Blew all my curls across my mouth.

    And, cool and sweet,
    My naked feet
Found dewy pathways through the wheat;
    And out again
    Where, down the lane,
The dust was dimpled with the rain.

"The song of yesterday"

II

But yesterday!—
Adream, astray,
From morning's red to evening's gray,
O'er dales and hills
Of daffodils
And lorn sweet-fluting whippoorwills.

I knew nor cares
Nor tears nor prayers—
A mortal god, crowned unawares
With sunset—and
A scepter-wand
Of apple-blossoms in my hand!

The dewy blue
Of twilight grew
To purple, with a star or two
Whose lisping rays
Failed in the blaze
Of sudden fireflys through the haze.

III

But yesterday
I heard the lay
Of summer birds, when I, as they
With breast and wing,
All quivering
With life and love, could only sing.

My head was leant
Where, with it, blent
A maiden's, o'er her instrument;
While all the night,
From vale to height,
Was filled with echoes of delight.

And all our dreams
Were lit with gleams
Of that lost land of reedy streams,
Along whose brim
Forever swim
Pan's lilies, laughing up at him.

IV

But yesterday! . . .
O blooms of May,
And summer roses—where away?
O stars above;
And lips of love,
And all the honeyed sweets thereof!—

O lad and lass,
And orchard pass,
And briered lane, and daisied grass!
O gleam and gloom,
And woodland bloom,
And breezy breaths of all perfume!—

No more for me
Or mine shall be
Thy raptures—save in memory,—
No more—no more—
Till through the Door
Of Glory gleam the days of yore.

AN END

GO away from me—do! I am tired of you!—
That I loved you last May isn't this season, too;
And, you know, every spring there's a new bird to
    sing
In the nest of the old, and a ghost on the wing!

Now, don't you assert that I'm simply a flirt—
And it's babyish for you to say that I hurt,
And my words are a dart, when they're only a part
Of your own fickle nature committed to heart.

It was all a mistake, and I don't want to make
The silly thing over for your silly sake—
Though I really once may have been such a dunce
As to fancy you loved me, some far-away months.

So, go away—do! I am tired clean through,
And you can't make me even feel sorry for you—
For, with us, every spring there's a new bird to sing
In the nest of the old, and a ghost on the wing.

HER CHOICE

"MY love or hate—choose which you
        will,"
He says; and o'er the window-sill
The rose-bush, jostled by the wind,
Rasps at his hands, close-clenched behind,
As she makes answer, smiling clear
As is the day,—"Your hate, my dear!"

An interval of silence—so
Intensely still, the cattle's low
Across the field's remotest rim
Comes like a near moan up to him,
While o'er the open sill once more
The rose-bush rasps him as before.

Then, with an impulse strange and new
To him, he says: "'Tis wise of you
To choose thus—for by such a choice
You lose so little, that,"—his voice
Breaks suddenly—the rose-bush stirs—
But ah! his hands are—safe in hers.

OUR OWN

THEY walk here with us, hand in hand;
    We gossip, knee by knee;
They tell us all that they have planned—
    Of all their joys to be,—
And, laughing, leave us: And, to-day,
    All desolate we cry
Across wide waves of voiceless graves—
    Good-by! Good-by! Good-by!

THE DRUM

O THE drum!
  There is some
    Intonation in thy grum
Monotony of utterance that strikes the spirit dumb,
As we hear
  Through the clear
    And unclouded atmosphere,
Thy palpitating syllables roll in upon the ear!

There's a part
  Of the art
    Of thy music-throbbing heart
That thrills a something in us that awakens with a
    start,
And in rhyme
  With the chime
    And exactitude of time,
Goes marching on to glory to thy melody sublime.

And the guest
  Of the breast
    That thy rolling robs of rest
Is a patriotic spirit as a Continental dressed;

And he looms
From the glooms
Of a century of tombs,
And the blood he spilled at Lexington in living
beauty blooms.

And his eyes
Wear the guise
Of a purpose pure and wise,
As the love of them is lifted to a something in the
skies
That is bright
Red and white,
With a blur of starry light,
As it laughs in silken ripples to the breezes day and
night.

There are deep
Hushes creep
O'er the pulses as they leap,
As thy tumult, fainter growing, on the silence falls
asleep,
While the prayer
Rising there
Wills the sea and earth and air
As a heritage to Freedom's sons and daughters
everywhere.

Then, with sound
As profound
As the thunderings resound,

Come thy wild reverberations in a throe that shakes
      the ground,
And a cry
    Flung on high,
        Like the flag it flutters by,
Wings rapturously upward till it nestles in the sky.

O the drum!
    There is some
        Intonation in thy grum
Monotony of utterance that strikes the spirit dumb,
As we hear,
    Through the clear
        And unclouded atmosphere,
Thy palpitating syllables roll in upon the ear!

A CASE IN P'INT

WE don't go much on lawin'
    Here in around the mines?—
Well, now, you're jest hurrahin'
  Like the wind amongst the pines!
Of course we allus aim to
  Give "the prisoner" a chance—
Though sometimes a jury's game to
  Ring a verdict in advance!

What wuz his name—this feller
  'At stold the Jedge's mare
Last spring?—wuz tryin' to sell her
  Down here at Rip and Tear,
When "Faro Bill" dropped on him,
  And bagged him, sound and good
And biznesslike, dog-gone him,
  As the constable a-could!

Well, anyway, his trial
  Wuz a case in p'int:—He pled
"Not guilty"—a denial
  'At his attorney said

Could be substantiated
  On the grounds, 'at when the mare
Wuz "stold," as claimed and stated,
  The defendant wuzn't square,—

But he'd be'n a testifyin',
  Round the raw edge of a spree
At Stutsman's bar, a-tryin'
  To hold one drink in three,
To "Jim-jams"; and he reckoned
  'At his client's moral tone
Could not be classed as second
  To the Jedge's—er his own.

"That savin'-clause is timely,"
  Says the Jedge, a-turnin' back
To color as sublimely
  As I've seed him turn a jack.—
"But," says he to the defendant,
  "Ef you didn't 'steal' the mare
I'll ask ef your attendant
  'Pharos William,' didn't swear

"You *wuzn't* 'full' when captured?"
  Then, a-drawin' of his gun,
The Jedge went on, enraptured
  With the trail 'at he'd begun,—
"I'll tax your re-collection
  To enquire ef you know
That hoss left my protection
  On'y jes' five hours ago?—

C—5

"In consequence, it follers,
  No man as drunk as you—
And I'll bet a hundred dollars
  To the opposition's two!—
Could sober to the beauty
  Of the standerd you present
This writin'—hence my duty
  Plainly is—to circumvent—"

And afore the jury knowed it,
  Bang! his gun went!—"And I'll ask,"
He went on, as he th'owed it
  Up to finish out his task,
"Ef it's mortal?"—then, betrayin'
  Some emotion, with a bow,
He closed by simply sayin'—
  "You can take the witness now!"

OLE BULL

DEAD; IN BERGEN, NORWAY; AUGUST 18, 1880

THE minstrel's mystic wand
　Has fallen from his hand;
　Stilled is the tuneful shell;
The airs he used to play
For us but yesterday
Have failed and died away
　In sad farewell.

Forgive—O noble heart,
Whose pure and gracious art
　Enraptured, all these years,
Sang sweet, and sweeter yet
Above all sounds that fret,
And all sobs of regret—
　Forgive our tears!

Forgive us, weeping thus
That thou art gone from us—
　Because thy song divine,
Too, with the master, gone,
Leaves us to listen on
In silence till the dawn
　That now is thine.

A WRAITH OF SUMMER-TIME

IN its color, shade and shine,
'Twas a summer warm as wine,
With an effervescent flavoring of flowered
bough and vine,
And a fragrance and a taste
Of ripe roses gone to waste,
And a dreamy sense of sun- and moon- and
starlight interlaced.

'Twas a summer such as broods
O'er enchanted solitudes,
Where the hand of Fancy leads us through
voluptuary moods,
And with lavish love outpours
All the wealth of out-of-doors,
And woos our feet o'er velvet paths and
honeysuckle floors.

'Twas a summer-time long dead,—
And its roses, white and red,
And its reeds and water-lilies down along
the river-bed,—
O they all are ghostly things—
For the ripple never sings,
And the rocking lily never even rustles as it
rings!

JACK THE GIANT-KILLER

Bad Boy's Version

TELL you a story—an' it's a fac':—
Wunst wuz a little boy, name wuz Jack,
An' he had sword an' buckle an' strap
Maked of gold, an' a " 'visibul cap";
An' he killed Gi'nts 'at et whole cows—
Th' horns an' all—an' pigs an' sows!
But Jack, his golding sword wuz, oh!
So awful sharp 'at he could go
An' cut th' ole Gi'nts clean in two
'Fore 'ey knowed what he wuz goin' to do!
An' *one* ole Gi'nt, he had four
Heads, an' name wuz "Bumblebore"—
An' he wuz feared o' Jack—'cause he,
Jack, he killed six—five—ten—three,
An' all o' th' uther ole Gi'nts but him:
An' thay wuz a place Jack haf to swim
'Fore he could git t' ole "Bumblebore"—
Nen thay wuz "griffuns" at the door:
But Jack, he thist plunged in an' swum
Clean acrost; an' when he come
To th' uther side, he thist put on

His " 'visibul cap," an' nen, dog-gone!
You couldn't see him at all!—An' so
He slewed the "griffuns"—*boff*, you know!
Nen wuz a horn hunged over his head,
High on th' wall, an' words 'at read,—
"Whoever kin this trumput blow
Shall cause the Gi'nt's overth'ow!"
An' Jack, he thist reached up an' blowed
The stuffin' out of it! an' th'owed
Th' castul gates wide open, an'
Nen tuk his gold sword in his han',
An' thist marched in t' ole "Bumblebore,"
An', 'fore he knowed, he put 'bout four
Heads on him—an' chopped 'em off, too!—
Wisht 'at *I'd* been Jack!—don't you?

REQUIESCAT

BE it life, be it death, there is nearing
    The dawn of a glorious day,
When the murmurs of doubt we are hearing
  In silence shall dwindle away;
And the hush and content that we covet—
  The rest that we need, and the sleep
That abides with the eyelids that love it,
  Shall come as we weep.

We shall listen no more to the sobbing
  Of sorrowing lips, and the sound
In our pillows at night of the throbbing
  Of feverish hearts will have found
The quiet beyond understanding,
  The rush and the moan of the rain,
That shall beat on the shingles, demanding
  Admittance in vain.

The hand on the dial shall number
  The hours unmarked; and the bell
Shall waken us not from the slumber
  That knows neither tolling of knell

Nor the peals of glad melody showered
  Like roses of song o'er the pave
Where the bride and the groom walk their
      flowered
  Green way to the grave.

In that dawn, when it breaks, we shall wonder
  No more why the heavens send back
To our prayers but the answer of thunder,
  And the lightning-scrawl, writ on the black
Of the storm in a language no mortal
  May read till his questioning sight
Shall have pierced through the innermost
      portal
  Of death to the light.

AT SEA

YEA, we go down to sea in ships—
   But Hope remains behind,
And Love, with laughter on his lips,
   And Peace, of passive mind;
While out across the deeps of night,
   With lifted sails of prayer,
We voyage off in quest of light,
   Nor find it anywhere.

O Thou who wroughtest earth and sea,
   Yet keepest from our eyes
The shores of an eternity
   In calms of Paradise,
Blow back upon our foolish quest
   With all the driving rain
Of blinding tears and wild unrest,
   And waft us home again!

SOMEP'N COMMON-LIKE

SOMEP'N 'at's common-like, and good
  And plain, and easy understood;
Somep'n 'at folks like me and you
Kin understand, and relish, too,
And find some sermint in 'at hits
The spot, and sticks and benefits.

We don't need nothin' extry fine;
'Cause, take the run o' minds like mine,
And we'll go more on good horse-sense
Than all your flowery eloquence;
And we'll jedge best of honest acts
By Nature's statement of the facts.

So when you're wantin' to express
Your misery, er happiness,
Er anything 'at's wuth the time
O' telling in plain talk er rhyme—
Jes' sort o' let your subject run
As ef the Lord wuz listenun.

BLIND

YOU think it is a sorry thing
    That I am blind. Your pitying
Is welcome to me; yet indeed,
I think I have but little need
Of it. Though you may marvel much
That *we,* who see by sense of touch
And taste and hearing, see things *you*
May never look upon; and true
Is it that even in the scent
Of blossoms *we* find something meant
No eyes have in their faces read,
Or wept to see interpreted.

And you might think it strange if now
I told you you were smiling. How
Do I know that? I hold your hand—
Its language I can understand—
Give both to me, and I will show
You many other things I know.
Listen: We never met before
Till now?—Well, you are something lower
Than five-feet-eight in height; and you
Are slender; and your eyes are blue —
Your mother's eyes—your mother's hair—

Your mother's likeness everywhere
Save in your walk—and that is quite
Your father's; nervous.—Am I right?
I thought so. And you used to sing,
But have neglected everything
Of vocalism—though you may
Still thrum on the guitar, and play
A little on the violin,—
I know that by the callus in
The finger-tips of your left hand—
And, by the by, though nature planned
You as most men, you are, I see,
"*Left*-handed," too,—the mystery
Is clear, though,—your right arm has been
Broken, to "break" the left one in.
And so, you see, though blind of sight,
I still have ways of seeing quite
Too well for you to sympathize
Excessively, with your good eyes.—
Though *once,* perhaps, to be sincere,
Within the whole asylum here,
From cupola to basement hall,
I was the blindest of them all!

Let us move farther down the walk—
The man here waiting hears my talk,
And is disturbed; besides, he may
Not be quite friendly anyway.
In fact—(this will be far enough;
Sit down)—the man just spoken of
Was once a friend of mine. He came

For treatment here from Burlingame—
A rich though brilliant student there,
Who read his eyes out of repair,
And groped his way up here, where we
Became acquainted, and where he
Met one of our girl-teachers, and,
If you'll believe me, asked her hand
In marriage, though the girl was blind
As I am—and the girl *declined*.
Odd, wasn't it? Look, you can see
Him waiting there. Fine, isn't he?
And handsome, eloquently wide
And high of brow, and dignified
With every outward grace, his sight
Restored to him, clear and bright
As day-dawn; waiting, waiting still
For the blind girl that never will
Be wife of his. How do I know?
You will recall a while ago
I told you he and I were friends.
In all that friendship comprehends,
I *was* his friend, I swear! why, now,
Remembering his love, and how
His confidence was all my own,
I hear, in fancy, the low tone
Of his deep voice, so full of pride
And passion, yet so pacified
With his affliction, that it seems
An utterance sent out of dreams
Of saddest melody, withal
So sorrowfully musical

It was, and is, must ever be—
But I'm digressing, pardon me.
I knew not anything of love
In those days, but of that above
All worldly passion,—for my art—
Music,—and that, with all my heart
And soul, blent in a love too great
For words of mine to estimate.
And though among my pupils she
Whose love my friend sought came to me,
I only knew her fingers' touch
Because they loitered overmuch
In simple scales, and needs must be
Untangled almost constantly.
But she was bright in other ways,
And quick of thought; with ready plays
Of wit, and with a voice as sweet
To listen to as one might meet
In any oratorio—
And once I gravely told her so,—
And, at my words, her limpid tone
Of laughter faltered to a moan,
And fell from that into a sigh
That quavered all so wearily,
That I, without the tear that crept
Between the keys, had known she wept;
And yet the hand I reached for then
She caught away, and laughed again.
And when that evening I strolled
With my old friend, I, smiling, told
Him I believed the girl and he

Were matched and mated perfectly:
He was so noble; she, so fair
Of speech, and womanly of air;
He, strong, ambitious; she, as mild
And artless even as a child;
And with a nature, I was sure,
As worshipful as it was pure
And sweet, and brimmed with tender things
Beyond his rarest fancyings.
He stopped me solemnly. He knew,
He said, how good, and just, and true
Was all I said of her; but as
For his own virtues, let them pass,
Since they were nothing to the one
That he had set his heart upon;
For but that morning she had turned
Forever from him. Then I learned
That for a month he had delayed
His going from us, with no aid
Of hope to hold him,—meeting still
Her ever-firm denial, till
Not even in his new-found sight
He found one comfort or delight.
And as his voice broke there, I felt
The brother-heart within me melt
In warm compassion for his own
That throbbed so utterly alone.
And then a sudden fancy hit
Along my brain; and coupling it
With a belief that I, indeed,
Might help my friend in his great need,

I warmly said that I would go
Myself, if he decided so,
And see her for him—that I knew
My pleadings would be listened to
Most seriously, and that she
Should love him, listening to me.
Go; bless me! And that was the last—
The last time his warm hand shut fast
Within my own—so empty since,
That the remembered finger-prints
I've kissed a thousand times, and wet
Them with the tears of all regret!

I know not how to rightly tell
How fared my quest, and what befell
Me, coming in the presence of
That blind girl, and her blinder love.
I know but little else than that
Above the chair in which she sat
I leant—reached for, and found her hand,
And held it for a moment, and
Took up the other—held them both—
As might a friend, I will take oath:
Spoke leisurely, as might a man
Praying for no thing other than
He thinks Heaven's justice:—She was blind,
I said, and yet a noble mind
Most truly loved her; one whose fond
Clear-sighted vision looked beyond
The bounds of her infirmity,
And saw the woman, perfectly

Modeled, and wrought out pure and true
And lovable.   She quailed, and drew
Her hands away, but closer still
I caught them.   "Rack me as you will!"
She cried out sharply—"Call me 'blind'—
Love ever is—I am resigned!
Blind is your friend; as blind as he
Am I—but blindest of the three—
Yea, blind as death—you will not see
My love for you is killing me!"

There is a memory that may
Not ever wholly fade away
From out my heart, so bright and fair
The light of it still glimmers there.
Why, it did seem as though my sight
Flamed back upon me, dazzling white
And godlike.   Not one other word
Of hers I listened for or heard,
But I *saw* songs sung in her eyes
Till they did swoon up drowning-wise,
As my mad lips did strike her own,
And we flashed one, and one alone!
Ah! was it treachery for me
To kneel there, drinking eagerly
That torrent-flow of words that swept
Out laughingly the tears she wept?—
Sweet words! O sweeter far, maybe,
Than light of day to those that see,—
God knows, who did the rapture send
To me, and hold it from my friend.

C—6

And we were married half a year
Ago.—And he is—waiting here,
Heedless of that—or anything,
But just that he is lingering
To say good-by to her, and bow—
As you may see him doing now,—
For there's her footstep in the hall;
God bless her!—help him!—save us all!

JUST AS OF OLD

JUST as of old! The world rolls on and on;
  The day dies into night—night into dawn—
Dawn into dusk—through centuries untold.—
        Just as of old.

Time loiters not. The river ever flows,
Its brink or white with blossoms or with snows;
Its tide or warm with spring or winter cold:
        Just as of old.

Lo! where is the beginning, where the end
Of living, loving, longing? *Listen,* friend!—
God answers with a silence of pure gold—
        Just as of old.

THE PRAYER PERFECT

DEAR Lord! kind Lord!
　　Gracious Lord! I pray
Thou wilt look on all I love,
　　Tenderly to-day!
Weed their hearts of weariness;
　　Scatter every care
Down a wake of angel-wings
　　Winnowing the air.

Bring unto the sorrowing
　　All release from pain;
Let the lips of laughter
　　Overflow again;
And with all the needy
　　O divide, I pray,
This vast treasure of content
　　That is mine to-day!

MONSIEUR LE SECRETAIRE

[JOHN CLARK RIDPATH]

MON cher Monsieur le Secretaire,
   Your song flits with me everywhere;
It lights on Fancy's prow and sings
Me on divinest voyagings:
And when my ruler love would fain
Be laid upon it—high again
It mounts, and hugs itself from me
With rapturous wings—still dwindlingly—
On!—on! till but a *ghost* is there
Of song, Monsieur le Secretaire!

A PHANTOM

LITTLE baby, you have wandered far away,
 And your fairy face comes back to me
  to-day,
 But I can not feel the strands
  Of your tresses, nor the play
 Of the dainty velvet-touches of your hands.

Little baby, you were mine to hug and hold;
Now your arms cling not about me as of old—
 O my dream of rest come true,
  And my richer wealth than gold,
 And the surest hope of Heaven that I knew!

O for the lisp long silent, and the tone
Of merriment once mingled with my own—
 For the laughter of your lips,
  And the kisses plucked and thrown
 In the lavish wastings of your finger-tips!

Little baby, O as then, come back to me,
And be again just as you used to be,
 For this phantom of you stands
  All too cold and silently,
 And will not kiss nor touch me with its hands.

WHAT REDRESS

I PRAY you, do not use this thing
  For vengeance; but if questioning
What wound, when dealt your humankind,
Goes deepest,—surely he will find
Who wrongs *you,* loving *him* no less—
There's nothing hurts like tenderness.

A LOST LOVE

'TWAS a summer ago when he left me here—
A summer of smiles, with never a tear
Till I said to him, with a sob, my dear,—
Good-by, my lover; good-by!

For I loved him, O as the stars love night!
And my cheeks for him flashed red and white
When first he called me his Heart's delight,—
Good-by, my lover; good-by!

The touch of his hand was a thing divine
As he sat with me in the soft moonshine
And drank of my love as men drink wine,—
Good-by, my lover; good-by!

And never a night as I knelt in prayer,
In thought as white as our own souls were,
But in fancy he came and he kissed me there,—
Good-by, my lover; good-by!

But now—ah, *now!* what an empty place
My whole heart is!—Of the old embrace
And the kiss I loved there lives no trace—
Good-by, my lover; good-by!

He sailed not over the stormy sea,
And he went not down in the waves—not he—
But O, he is lost—for he married me—
    Good-by, my lover; good-by!

LET US FORGET

LET us forget. What matters it that we
  Once reigned o'er happy realms of long ago,
  And talked of love, and let our voices low,
And ruled for some brief sessions royally?
What if we sung, or laughed, or wept maybe?
  It has availed not anything, and so
  Let it go by that we may better know
How poor a thing is lost to you and me.
  But yesterday I kissed your lips, and yet
Did thrill you not enough to shake the dew
  From your drenched lids—and missed, with no
      regret,
Your kiss shot back, with sharp breaths failing
    you:
  And so, to-day, while our worn eyes are wet
  With all this waste of tears, let us forget!

THE SHOEMAKER

THOU Poet, who, like any lark,
  Dost whet thy beak and trill
From misty morn till murky dark,
  Nor ever pipe thy fill:
Hast thou not, in thy cheery note,
  One poor chirp to confer—
One verseful twitter to devote
  Unto the Shoe-ma-ker?

At early dawn he doth peg in
  His noble work and brave;
And eke from cark and worldly sin
  He seeketh soles to save;
And all day long, with quip and song,
  Thus stitcheth he the way
Our feet may know the right from wrong
  Nor ever go astray.

Soak kip in mind the Shoe-ma-ker,
  Nor slight his lasting fame:
Alway he waxeth tenderer
  In warmth of our acclaim;—-

Ay, more than any artisan
　　We glory in his art
Who ne'er, to help the under man,
　　Neglects the upper part.

But toe the mark for him, and heel
　　Respond to thee in kine—
Or kid—or calf, shouldst thou reveal
　　A taste so superfine:
Thus let him jest—join in his laugh—
　　Draw on his stock, and be
A shoer'd there's no rival half-
　　Sole liberal as he.

Then, Poet, hail the Shoe-ma-ker
　　For all his goodly deeds,—
Yea, bless him free for booting thee—
　　The first of all thy needs!
And when at last his eyes grow dim,
　　And nerveless drops his clamp,
In golden shoon pray think of him
　　Upon his latest tramp.

IN THE CORRIDOR

AH! at last alone, love!
   Now the band may play
Till its sweetest tone, love,
   Swoons and dies away!
They who most will miss us
   We're not caring for—
Who of them could kiss us
   In the corridor?

Had we only known, dear,
   Ere this long delay,
Just how all alone, dear,
   We might waltz away,
Then for hours, like this, love,
   We are longing for,
We'd have still to kiss, love,
   In the corridor!

Nestle in my heart, love;
   Hug and hold me close—
Time will come to part, love,
   Ere a fellow knows;
There! the Strauss is ended—
   Whirl across the floor,
Isn't waltzing splendid
   In the corridor?

SUSPENSE

A WOMAN'S figure, on a ground of night
   Inlaid with sallow stars that dimly stare
  Down in the lonesome eyes, uplifted there
As in vague hope some alien lance of light
Might pierce their woe. The tears that blind her
     sight—
  The salt and bitter blood of her despair—
  Her hands toss back through torrents of her
     hair
And grip toward God with anguish infinite.
  And O the carven mouth, with all its great
Intensity of longing frozen fast
  In such a smile as well may designate
The slowly murdered heart, that, to the last,
  Conceals each newer wound, and back at Fate
  Throbs Love's eternal lie—"Lo, I can wait!"

A NONSENSE RHYME

RINGLETY-JING!
  And what will we sing?
Some little crinkety-crankety thing
    That rhymes and chimes,
    And skips, sometimes,
As though wound up with a kink in the spring.

     Grunkety-krung!
     And chunkety-plung!
Sing the song that the bullfrog sung,—
       A song of the soul
       Of a mad tadpole
     That met his fate in a leaky bowl:
And it's O for the first false wiggle he made
In a sea of pale pink lemonade!
      And it's O for the thirst
        Within him pent,
      And the hopes that burst
        As his reason went—
When his strong arm failed and his strength was
    spent!

Sing, O sing
Of the things that cling,
And the claws that clutch and the fangs that
        sting—
            Till the tadpole's tongue
            And his tail upflung
Quavered and failed with a song unsung!
            O the dank despair in the rank morass,
            Where the crawfish crouch in the cring-
                ing grass,
        And the long limp rune of the loon wails on
            For the mad, sad soul
            Of a bad tadpole
                Forever lost and gone!

        Jinglety-jee!
    And now we'll see
What the last of the lay shall be,
        As the dismal tip of the tune, O friends,
        Swoons away and the long tale ends.
            And it's O and alack!
                For the tangled legs
            And the spangled back
                Of the green grig's eggs,
            And the unstrung strain
            Of the strange refrain
That the winds wind up like a strand of rain!

            And it's O,
                Also,
        For the ears wreathed low,

Like a laurel-wreath on the lifted brow
Of the frog that chants of the why and how,
    And the wherefore too, and the thus and so
    Of the wail he weaves in a woof of woe!
Twangle, then, with your wrangling strings,
The tinkling links of a thousand things!
And clang the pang of a maddening moan
Till the Echo, hid in a land unknown,
    Shall leap as he hears, and hoot and hoo
    Like the wretched wraith of a Whoopty-
        Doo!

LOUELLA WAINIE

LOUELLA WAINIE! where are you?
  Do you not hear me as I cry?
Dusk is falling; I feel the dew;
  And the dark will be here by and by:
    I hear no thing but the owl's hoo-hoo!
    Louella Wainie! where are you?

Hand in hand to the pasture bars
  We came loitering, Lou and I,
Long ere the fireflies coaxed the stars
  Out of their hiding-place on high.
    O how sadly the cattle moo!
    Louella Wainie! where are you?

Laughingly we parted here—
  "I will go this way," said she,
"And you will go that way, my dear"—
  Kissing her dainty hand at me—
    And the hazels hid her from my view.
    Louella Wainie! where are you?

Is there ever a sadder thing
  Than to stand on the farther brink
Of twilight, hearing the marsh-frogs sing?

Nothing could sadder be, I think!
  And ah! how the night-fog chills one
      through.
  Louella Wainie! where are you?

Water-lilies and oozy leaves—
  Lazy bubbles that bulge and stare
Up at the moon through the gloom it weaves
  Out of the willows waving there!
    Is it despair I am wading through?
    Louella Wainie! where are you?

Louella Wainie, listen to me,
  Listen, and send me some reply,
For so will I call unceasingly
  Till death shall answer me by and by—
    Answer, and help me to find you too
    Louella Wainie! where are you?

FOR YOU

FOR you, I could forget the gay
   Delirium of merriment,
And let my laughter die away
   In endless silence of content.
     I could forget, for your dear sake,
     The utter emptiness and ache
     Of every loss I ever knew.—
     What could I not forget for you?

I could forget the just deserts
   Of mine own sins, and so erase
The tear that burns, the smile that hurts,
   And all that mars and masks my face.
     For your fair sake I could forget
     The bonds of life that chafe and fret,
     Nor care if death were false or true.—
     What could I not forget for you?

What could I not forget? Ah me!
   One thing I know would still abide
Forever in my memory,
   Though all of love were lost beside—
     I yet would feel how first the wine
     Of your sweet lips made fools of mine
     Until they sung, all drunken through—
     "What could I not forget for you?"

MY FIRST SPECTACLES

AT first I laughed—for it was quite
   An oddity to see
My reflex looking from the glass
   Through spectacles at me.

But as I gazed I really found
   They so improved my sight
That many wrinkles in my face
   Were mixed with my delight;

And many streaks of silver, too,
   Were gleaming in my hair,
With quite a hint of baldness that
   I never dreamed was there.

And as I readjusted them
   And winked in slow surprise,
A something like a mist had come
   Between them and my eyes.

And, peering vainly still, the old
   Optician said to me,
The while he took them from my nose
   And wiped them hastily:

"Jes' now, of course, your eyes is apt
   To water some—but where
Is any man's on earth that won't
   The first he has to wear?"

THE TEXT

THE text: Love thou thy fellow man!
    He may have sinned;—One proof in-
        deed,
He is thy fellow, reach thy hand
    And help him in his need!

Love thou thy fellow man. He may
    Have wronged thee—then, the less excuse
Thou hast for wronging him. Obey
    What he has dared refuse!

Love thou thy fellow man—for, be
    His life a light or heavy load,
No less he needs the love of thee
    To help him on his road.

AN OUT-WORN SAPPHO

HOW tired I am! I sink down all alone
   Here by the wayside of the Present. Lo,
Even as a child I hide my face and moan—
  A little girl that may no farther go:
  The path above me only seems to grow
    More rugged, climbing still, and ever briered
  With keener thorns of pain than these below;
  And O the bleeding feet that falter so
    And are so very tired!

Why, I have journeyed from the far-off Lands
  Of Babyhood—where baby-lilies blew
Their trumpets in mine ears, and filled my hands
  With treasures of perfume and honey-dew,
  And where the orchard shadows ever drew
    Their cool arms round me when my cheeks
        were fired
  With too much joy, and lulled mine eyelids to,
  And only let the starshine trickle through
    In sprays, when I was tired!

Yet I remember, when the butterfly
  Went flickering about me like a flame

That quenched itself in roses suddenly,
  How oft I wished that *I* might blaze the same,
  And in some rose-wreath nestle with my name,
    While all the world looked on it and admired.—
  Poor moth!—Along my wavering flight toward
      fame
  The winds drive backward, and my wings are
      lame
      And broken, bruised and tired!

I hardly know the path from those old times;
  I know at first it was a smoother one
Than this that hurries past me now, and climbs
  So high, its far cliffs even hide the sun
  And shroud in gloom my journey scarce begun.
    I could not do quite all the world required—
  I could not do quite all I should have done,
  And in my eagerness I have outrun
      My strength—and I am tired. . . .

Just tired! But when of old I had the stay
  Of mother-hands, O very sweet indeed
It was to dream that all the weary way
  I should but follow where I now must lead—
  For long ago they left me in my need,
    And, groping on alone, I tripped and mired
  Among rank grasses where the serpents breed
  In knotted coils about the feet of speed.—
      There first it was I tired.

And yet I staggered on, and bore my load
  Right gallantly: The sun, in summer-time,
In lazy belts came slipping down the road
  To woo me on, with many a glimmering rhyme
  Rained from the golden rim of some fair clime,
    That, hovering beyond the clouds, inspired
  My failing heart with fancies so sublime
  I half forgot my path of dust and grime,
    Though I was growing tired.

And there were many voices cheering me:
  I listened to sweet praises where the wind
Went laughing o'er my shoulders gleefully
  And scattering my love-songs far behind;—
  Until, at last, I thought the world so kind—
    So rich in all my yearning soul desired—
  So generous—so loyally inclined,
  I grew to love and trust it. . . . I was blind—
    Yea, blind as I was tired!

And yet one hand held me in creature-touch:
  And O, how fain it was, how true and strong,
How it did hold my heart up like a crutch,
  Till, in my dreams, I joyed to walk along
  The toilsome way, contented with a song—
    'Twas all of earthly things I had acquired,
  And 'twas enough, I feigned, or right or wrong,
  Since, binding me to man—a mortal thong—
    It stayed me, growing tired. . . .

Yea, I had e'en resigned me to the strait
  Of earthly rulership—had bowed my head
Acceptant of the master-mind—the great
  One lover—lord of all,—the perfected
  Kiss-comrade of my soul;—had stammering said
    My prayers to him;—all—all that he desired
I rendered sacredly as we were wed.—
  Nay—nay!—'twas but a myth I worshipèd.—
    And—God of love!—how tired!

For, O my friends, to lose the latest grasp—
  To feel the last hope slipping from its hold—
To feel the one fond hand within your clasp
  Fall slack, and loosen with a touch so cold
  Its pressure may not warm you as of old
    Before the light of love had thus expired—
  To know your tears are worthless, though they
      rolled
  Their torrents out in molten drops of gold.—
    God's pity! I am tired!

And I must rest.—Yet do not say "She *died*,"
  In speaking of me, sleeping here alone.
I kiss the grassy grave I sink beside,
  And close mine eyes in slumber all mine own:
  Hereafter I shall neither sob nor moan
    Nor murmur one complaint;—all I desired,
  And failed in life to find, will now be known—
  So let me dream.   Good night! And on the stone
    Say simply: She was tired.

'Tis all to ask

WILLIAM BROWN

"HE bore the name of William Brown"—
  His name, at least, did not go down
  With him that day
  He went the way
  Of certain death where duty lay.

He looked his fate full in the face—
He saw his watery resting-place
  Undaunted, and
  With firmer hand
  Held others' hopes in sure command.—

The hopes of full three hundred lives—
Aye, babes unborn, and promised wives!
  "The odds are dread,"
  He must have said,
  "Here, God, is one poor life instead."

No time for praying overmuch—
No time for tears, or woman's touch
  Of tenderness,
  Or child's caress—
  His last "God bless them!" stopped at
      "bless"—

671

Thus man and engine, nerved with steel,
Clasped iron hands for woe or weal,
   And so went down
   Where dark waves drown
All but the name of William Brown.

THE NINE LITTLE GOBLINS

THEY all climbed up on a high board-fence—
   Nine little goblins, with green-glass eyes—
Nine little goblins that had no sense,
  And couldn't tell coppers from cold mince pies;
    And they all climbed up on the fence, and sat—
    And I asked them what they were staring at.

And the first one said, as he scratched his head
  With a queer little arm that reached out of his ear
And rasped its claws in his hair so red—
   "This is what this little arm is fer!"
    And he scratched and stared, and the next one
     said,
    "How on earth do *you* scratch your head?"

And he laughed like the screech of a rusty hinge—
  Laughed and laughed till his face grew black;
And when he choked, with a final twinge
  Of his stifling laughter, he thumped his back
    With a fist that grew on the end of his tail
    Till the breath came back to his lips so pale.

And the third little goblin leered round at me—
  And there were no lids on his eyes at all,—
And he clucked one eye, and he says, says he,
  "What is the style of your socks this fall?"
    And he clapped his heels—and I sighed to see
    That he had hands where his feet should be.

673

Then a bald-faced goblin, gray and grim,
  Bowed his head, and I saw him slip
His eyebrows off, as I looked at him,
    And paste them over his upper lip;
      And then he moaned in remorseful pain—
      "Would—Ah, would I'd me brows again!"

And then the whole of the goblin band
  Rocked on the fence-top to and fro,
And clung, in a long row, hand in hand,
    Singing the songs that they used to know—
      Singing the songs that their grandsires sung
      In the goo-goo days of the goblin-tongue.

And ever they kept their green-glass eyes
  Fixed on me with a stony stare—
Till my own grew glazed with a dread surmise,
    And my hat whooped up on my lifted hair,
      And I felt the heart in my breast snap to,
      As you've heard the lid of a snuff-box do.

And they sang: "You're asleep! There is no board-
        fence,
  And never a goblin with green-glass eyes!—
'Tis only a vision the mind invents
    After a supper of cold mince pies.—
      And you're doomed to dream this way," they
        said,—
      *"And you shan't wake up till you're clean
        plum dead!"*

WHY

WHY are they written—all these lovers'
    rhymes?
 I catch faint perfumes of the blossoms white
 That maidens drape their tresses with at night,
 And, through dim smiles of beauty and the din
 Of the musicians' harp and violin,
 I hear, enwound and blended with the dance,
 The voice whose echo is this utterance,—
Why are they written—all these lovers' rhymes?

Why are they written—all these lovers' rhymes?
 I see but vacant windows, curtained o'er
 With webs whose architects forevermore
 Race up and down their slender threads to bind
 The buzzing fly's wings whirless, and to wind
 The living victim in his winding sheet.—
 I shudder, and with whispering lips repeat,
Why are they written—all these lovers' rhymes?

Why are they written—all these lovers' rhymes?
 What will you have for answer?—Shall I say
 That he who sings the merriest roundelay
 Hath neither joy nor hope?—and he who sings
 The lightest, sweetest, tenderest of things
 But utters moan on moan of keenest pain,
 So aches his heart to ask and ask in vain,
Why are they written—all these lovers' rhymes?

THE TOUCH OF LOVING HANDS
IMITATED

LIGHT falls the rain-drop on the fallen leaf,
  And light o'er harvest-plain and garnered
   sheaf—
  But lightlier falls the touch of loving hands.

Light falls the dusk of mild midsummer night,
And light the first star's faltering lance of light
  On glimmering lawns,—but lightlier loving
   hands.

And light the feathery flake of early snows,
Or wisp of thistle-down that no wind blows,
  And light the dew,—but lightlier loving hands.

Light-falling dusk, or dew, or summer rain,
Or down of snow or thistle—all are vain,—
  Far lightlier falls the touch of loving hands.

THE OLD SCHOOL-CHUM

HE puts the poem by, to say
 His eyes are not themselves to-day!

A sudden glamour o'er his sight—
A something vague, indefinite—

An oft-recurring blur that blinds
The printed meaning of the lines,

And leaves the mind all dusk and dim
In swimming darkness—strange to him!

It is not childishness, I guess,—
Yet something of the tenderness

That used to wet his lashes when
A boy seems troubling him again;—

The old emotion, sweet and wild,
That drove him truant when a child,

That he might hide the tears that fell
Above the lesson—"Little Nell."

And so it is he puts aside
The poem he has vainly tried

To follow; and, as one who sighs
In failure, through a poor disguise

Of smiles, he dries his tears, to say
His eyes are not themselves to-day.

A CUP OF TEA

I HAVE sipped, with drooping lashes,
  Dreamy draughts of Verzenay;
I have flourished brandy-smashes
  In the wildest sort of way;
I have joked with "Tom and Jerry"
  Till "wee hours ayont the twal"—
But I've found my tea the very
  Safest tipple of them all!

'Tis a mystical potation
  That exceeds in warmth of glow
And divine exhilaration
  All the drugs of long ago—
All of old magicians' potions—
  Of Medea's philtered spells—
Or of fabled isles and oceans
  Where the Lotos-eater dwells!

Though I've reveled o'er late lunches
  With blasé dramatic stars,
And absorbed their wit and punches
  And the fumes of their cigars—

Drank in the latest story,
  With a cocktail either end,—
I have drained a deeper glory
  In a cup of tea, my friend.

Green, Black, Moyune, Formosa,
  Congou, Amboy, Pingsuey—
No odds the name it knows—ah,
  Fill a cup of it for me!
And, as I clink my china
  Against your goblet's brim,
My tea in steam shall twine a
  Fragrant laurel round its rim.

TO THE SERENADER

TINKLE on, O sweet guitar,
   Let the dancing fingers
Loiter where the low notes are
   Blended with the singer's:
Let the midnight pour the moon's
   Mellow wine of glory
Down upon him through the tune's
   Old romantic story!

I am listening, my love,
   Through the cautious lattice,
Wondering why the stars above
   All are blinking at us;
Wondering if his eyes from there
   Catch the moonbeam's shimmer
As it lights the robe I wear
   With a ghostly glimmer.

Lilt thy song, and lute away
   In the wildest fashion:—
Pour thy rippling roundelay
   O'er the heights of passion!—
Flash it down the fretted strings
   Till 'thy mad lips, missing
All but smothered whisperings,
   Press this rose I'm kissing.

WHAT A DEAD MAN SAID

HEAR what a dead man said to me.
His lips moved not, and the eyelids lay
Shut as the leaves of a white rose may
Ere the wan bud blooms out perfectly;
And the lifeless hands they were stiffly crossed
As they always cross them over the breast
When the soul goes nude and the corpse is dressed;
And over the form, in its long sleep lost,
From forehead down to the pointed feet
That peaked the foot of the winding-sheet,
Pallid patience and perfect rest.—
It was the voice of a dream, may be,
But it seemed that the dead man said to me:
"I, indeed, am the man that died
Yesternight—and you weep for this;
But, lo, I am with you, side by side,
As we have walked when the summer sun
Made the smiles of our faces one,
And touched our lips with the same warm kiss.
Do not doubt that I tell you true—
I am the man you once called friend,
And caught my hand when I came to you,
And loosed it only because the end

Of the path I walked of a sudden stopped—
And a dead man's hand must needs be dropped—
And I—though it's strange to think so now—
I have wept, as you weep for me,
And pressed hot palms to my aching brow
And moaned through the long night ceaselessly.

Yet have I lived to forget my pain,
As you will live to be glad again—
Though never so glad as this hour am I,
Tasting a rapture of delight
Vast as the heavens are infinite,
And dear as the hour I came to die.
Living and loving, I dreamed my cup
Brimmed sometimes, and with marvelings
I have lifted and tipped it up
And drunk to the dregs of all sweet things.
Living, 'twas but a *dream* of bliss—
Now I *realize* all it is;
And now my only shadow of grief
Is that I may not give relief
Unto those living and dreaming on,
And woo them graveward, as I have gone,
And show death's loveliness,—for they
Shudder and shrink as they walk this way,
Never dreaming that all they dread
Is their purest delight when dead."

Thus it was, or it seemed to be,
That the voice of the dead man spoke to me.

A TEST

'TWAS a test I designed, in a quiet conceit
   Of myself, and the thoroughly fixed and com-
       plete
Satisfaction I felt in the utter control
Of the guileless young heart of the girl of my soul.

So—we parted. I said it were better we should—
That she could forget me—I knew that she could;
For I never was worthy so tender a heart,
And so for her sake it were better to part.

She averted her gaze, and she sighed and looked sad
As I held out my hand—for the ring that she had—
With the bitterer speech that I hoped she might be
Resigned to look up and be happy with me.

'Twas a test, as I said—but God pity your grief,
At a moment like this when a smile of relief
Shall leap to the lips of the woman you prize,
And no mist of distress in her glorious eyes.

A SONG FOR CHRISTMAS

CHANT me a rhyme of Christmas—
   Sing me a jovial song,—
And though it is filled with laughter,
   Let it be pure and strong.

Let it be clear and ringing,
   And though it mirthful be,
Let a low, sweet voice of pathos
   Run through the melody.

Sing of the hearts brimmed over
   With the story of the day—
Of the echo of childish voices
   That will not die away.—

Of the blare of the tasseled bugle,
   And the timeless clatter and beat
Of the drum that throbs to muster
   Squadrons of scampering feet.

But O let your voice fall fainter,
   Till, blent with a minor tone,
You temper your song with the beauty
   Of the pity Christ hath shown:

And sing one verse for the voiceless;
  And yet, ere the song be done,
A verse for the ears that hear not,
  And a verse for the sightless one:

For though it be time for singing
  A merry Christmas glee,
Let a low, sweet voice of pathos
  Run through the melody.

SUN AND RAIN

ALL day the sun and rain have been as friends,
Each vying with the other which shall be
Most generous in dowering earth and sea
With their glad wealth, till each, as it descends,
Is mingled with the other, where it blends
In one warm, glimmering mist that falls on me
As once God's smile fell over Galilee.
The lily-cup, filled with it, droops and bends
Like some white saint beside a sylvan shrine
In silent prayer; the roses at my feet,
Baptized with it as with a crimson wine,
Gleam radiant in grasses grown so sweet,
The blossoms lift, with tenderness divine,
Their wet eyes heavenward with these of mine.

WITH HER FACE

WITH her face between his hands!
   Was it any wonder she
   Stood atiptoe tremblingly?
As his lips along the strands
Of her hair went lavishing
Tides of kisses, such as swing
Love's arms to like iron bands.—
With her face between his hands!

And the hands—the hands that pressed
   The glad face—Ah! where are they?
   Folded limp, and laid away
Idly over idle breast?
He whose kisses drenched her hair,
As he caught and held her there,
In Love's alien, lost lands,
With her face between his hands?

Was it long and long ago,
   When her face was not as now,
   Dim with tears? nor wan her brow
As a winter-night of snow?
Nay, anointing still the strands
Of her hair, his kisses flow
Flood-wise, as she dreaming stands,
With her face between his hands.

MY NIGHT

HUSH! hush! list, heart of mine, and hearken
        low!
  You do not guess how tender is the Night,
  And in what faintest murmurs of delight
Her deep, dim-throated utterances flow
Across the memories of long-ago!
  Hark! do your senses catch the exquisite
  Staccatos of a bird that dreams he sings?
Nay, then, you hear not rightly,—'tis a blur
  Of misty love-notes, laughs and whisperings
The Night pours o'er the lips that fondle her,
  And that faint breeze, filled with all fragrant
        sighs,—
  That is her breath that quavers lover-wise—
O blessed sweetheart, with thy swart, sweet kiss,
Baptize me, drown me in black swirls of bliss!

THE HOUR BEFORE THE DAWN

THE hour before the dawn!
 O ye who grope therein, with fear and
  dread
And agony of soul, be comforted,
Knowing, ere long, the darkness will be gone,
 And down its dusky aisles the light be shed;
Therefore, in utter trust, fare on—fare on,
 This hour before the dawn!

THE OLD YEAR AND THE NEW

I

AS one in sorrow looks upon
  The dead face of a loyal friend,
By the dim light of New Year's dawn
  I saw the Old Year end.

Upon the pallid features lay
  The dear old smile—so warm and bright
Ere thus its cheer had died away
  In ashes of delight.

The hands that I had learned to love
  With strength of passion half divine,
Were folded now, all heedless of
  The emptiness of mine.

The eyes that once had shed their bright
  Sweet looks like sunshine, now were dull,
And ever lidded from the light
  That made them beautiful.

II

The chimes of bells were in the air,
  And sounds of mirth in hall and street,
With pealing laughter everywhere
  And throb of dancing feet:

The mirth and the convivial din
  Of revelers in wanton glee,
With tunes of harp and violin
  In tangled harmony.

But with a sense of nameless dread,
  I turned me, from the merry face
Of this newcomer, to my dead;
  And, kneeling there a space,

I sobbed aloud, all tearfully:—
  By this dear face so fixed and cold,
O Lord, let not this New Year be
  As happy as the old!

GOOD-BY, OLD YEAR

GOOD-BY, Old Year!
              Good-by!
We have been happy—you and I;
   We have been glad in many ways;
And now, that you have come to die,
   Remembering our happy days,
'Tis hard to say, "Good-by—
   Good-by, Old Year!
              Good-by!"

Good-by, Old Year!
              Good-by!
We have seen sorrow—you and I—
   Such hopeless sorrow, grief and care,
That now, that you have come to die,
   Remembering our old despair,
'Tis sweet to say, "Good-by—
   Good-by, Old Year!
              Good-by!"

AS CREATED

THERE'S a space for good to bloom in
    Every heart of man or woman,—
And however wild or human,
    Or however brimmed with gall,
Never heart may beat without it;
And the darkest heart to doubt it
Has something good about it
        After all.

SOMEDAY

SOMEDAY:—So many tearful eyes
  Are watching for thy dawning light;
So many faces toward the skies
  Are weary of the night!

So many failing prayers that reel
  And stagger upward through the storm,
And yearning hands that reach and feel
  No pressure true and warm.

So many hearts whose crimson wine
  Is wasted to a purple stain
And blurred and streaked with drops of brine
  Upon the lips of Pain.

Oh, come to them!—these weary ones!
  Or if thou still must bide a while,
Make stronger yet the hope that runs
  Before thy coming smile:

And haste and find them where they wait—
  Let summer-winds blow down that way,
And all they long for, soon or late,
  Bring round to them, Someday.

FALSE AND TRUE

ONE said: "Here is my hand to lean upon
　　As long as you may need it." And one said:
　"Believe me true to you till I am dead."
And one, whose dainty way it was to fawn
About my face, with mellow fingers drawn
　　Most soothingly o'er brow and drooping head,
　　Sighed tremulously: "Till my breath is fled
Know I am faithful!" . . . Now, all these are gone
　　And many like to them—and yet I make
No bitter moan above their grassy graves—
　　Alas! they are not dead for me to take
Such sorry comfort!—but my heart behaves
　　Most graciously, since one who never spake
　　A vow is true to me for true love's sake.

A BALLAD FROM APRIL

I AM dazed and bewildered with living
　　A life but an intricate skein
Of hopes and despairs and thanksgiving
　. Wound up and unraveled again—
Till it seems, whether waking or sleeping,
　　I am wondering ever the while
At a something that smiles when I'm weeping,
　　And a something that weeps when I smile.

And I walk through the world as one dreaming
　　Who knows not the night from the day,
For I look on the stars that are gleaming,
　　And lo, they have vanished away:
And I look on the sweet-summer daylight,
　　And e'en as I gaze it is fled,
And, veiled in a cold, misty, gray light,
　　The winter is there in its stead.

I feel in my palms the warm fingers
　　Of numberless friends—and I look,
And lo, not a one of them lingers
　　To give back the pleasure he took;

And I lift my sad eyes to the faces
 All tenderly fixed on my own,
But they wither away in grimaces
 That scorn me, and leave me alone.

And I turn to the woman that told me
 Her love would live on until death—
But her arms they no longer enfold me,
 Though barely the dew of her breath
Is dry on the forehead so pallid
 That droops like the weariest thing
O'er this most inharmonious ballad
 That ever a sorrow may sing.

So I'm dazed and bewildered with living
 A life but an intricate skein
Of hopes and despairs and thanksgiving
 Wound up and unraveled again—
Till it seems, whether waking or sleeping,
 I am wondering ever the while
At a something that smiles when I'm weeping
 And a something that weeps when I smile.

WHEN DE FOLKS IS GONE

WHAT dat scratchin' at de kitchen do'?
   Done heah'n dat foh an hour er mo'!
Tell you, Mr. Niggah, das sho's you' bo'n,
Hit's mighty lonesome waitin' when de folks is
      gone!

Blame my trap! how de wind do blow!
An' dis is das de night foh de witches, sho'!
Dey's trouble gon' to waste when de old slut whine,
An' you heah de cat a-spittin' when de moon don't
      shine!

Chune my fiddle, an' de bridge go *"bang!"*
An' I lef' 'er right back whah she allus hang,
An' de tribble snap short an' de apern split
When dey no mortal man wah a-tetchin' hit!

Dah! *Now,* what? How de ole j'ice cracks!
'Spec' dis house, ef hit tell plain fac's,
'Ud talk about de ha'nts wid dey long tails on
What das'n't on'y come when de folks is gone!

What I tuk an' done ef a sho'-'nuff ghos'
Pop right up by de ole bed-pos'?
What dat shinin' fru de front do' crack? . . .
God bress de Lo'd! hit's de folks got back!

THE TWINS

ONE'S the pictur' of his Pa,
 And the *other* of her Ma—
Jes' the bossest pair o' babies 'at a mortal
  ever saw!
And we love 'em as the bees
Loves the blossoms on the trees,
A-ridin' and a-rompin' in the breeze!

One's got her Mammy's eyes—
Soft and blue as Apurl-skies—
With the same sort of a *smile,* like—Yes,
  and mouth about her size,—
Dimples, too, in cheek and chin,
'At my lips jes' *wallers* in,
A-goin' to work, er gittin' home ag'in.

And the *other*—Well, they say
That he's got his Daddy's way
O' bein' ruther soberfied, er ruther extry
  gay,—
That he eether cries his best,
Er he laughs his howlin'est—
Like all he lacked was buttons and a vest!

700

Look at *her!*—and look at *him!*—
Talk about yer "Cheru-*bim!*"
Roll 'em up in dreams together, rosy arm
   and chubby limb!
O we love 'em as the bees
Loves the blossoms on the trees,
A-ridin' and a-rompin' in the breeze!

THE ORCHARD LANDS OF LONG AGO

THE orchard lands of Long Ago!
  O drowsy winds, awake, and blow
The snowy blossoms back to me,
And all the buds that used to be!
Blow back along the grassy ways
Of truant feet, and lift the haze
Of happy summer from the trees
That trail their tresses in the seas
Of grain that float and overflow
The orchard lands of Long Ago!

Blow back the melody that slips
In lazy laughter from the lips
That marvel much if any kiss
Is sweeter than the apple's is.
Blow back the twitter of the birds—
The lisp, the titter, and the words
Of merriment that found the shine
Of summer-time a glorious wine
That drenched the leaves that loved it so,
In orchard lands of Long Ago!

O memory! alight and sing
Where rosy-bellied pippins cling,
And golden russets glint and gleam,
As, in the old Arabian dream,
The fruits of that enchanted tree
The glad Aladdin robbed for me!
And, drowsy winds, awake and fan
My blood as when it overran
A heart ripe as the apples grow
In orchard lands of Long Ago!

BRUDDER SIMS

DAH'S Brudder Sims! Dast slam yo' Bible shet
      An' lef' dat man alone—kase he's de boss
    Ob all de preachahs ev' I come across!
Day's no twis' in dat gospil book, I bet,
Ut Brudder Sims cain't splanify, an' set
      You' min' at eaze! W'at's Moses an' de Laws?
      W'at's fo'ty days an' nights ut Noey toss
Aroun' de Dil-ooge?—W'at dem Chillen et
    De Lo'd rain down? W'at s'prise ole Joney so
In dat whale's inna'ds?—W'at dat laddah mean
      Ut Jacop see?—an' wha' dat laddah go?—
Who clim dat laddah?—Wha' dat laddah lean?—
      An' wha' dat laddah now? "Dast chalk yo' toe
      Wid Faith," sez Brudder Sims, "an' den you
        know!"

DEFORMED

CROUCHED at the corner of the street
  She sits all day, with face too white
And hands too wasted to be sweet
  In anybody's sight.

Her form is shrunken, and a pair
  Of crutches leaning at her side
Are crossed like homely hands in prayer
  At quiet eventide.

Her eyes—two lustrous, weary things—
  Have learned a look that ever aches,
Despite the ready jinglings
  The passer's penny makes.

And, noting this, I pause and muse
  If any precious promise touch
This heart that has so much to lose
  If dreaming overmuch—

And, in a vision, mistily
  Her future womanhood appears,—
A picture framed with agony
  And drenched with ceaseless tears—

705

Where never lover comes to claim
  The hand outheld so yearningly—
The laughing babe that lisps her name
  Is but a fantasy!

And, brooding thus, all swift and wild
  A daring fancy, strangely sweet,
Comes o'er me, that the crippled child
  That crouches at my feet—

Has found her head a resting-place
  Upon my shoulder, while my kiss
Across the pallor of her face
  Leaves crimson trails of bliss.

WHILE THE MUSICIAN PLAYED

O IT was but a dream I had
　　While the musician played!—
And here the sky, and here the glad
　　Old ocean kissed the glade;
And here the laughing ripples ran,
　　And here the roses grew
That threw a kiss to every man
　　That voyaged with the crew.

Our silken sails in lazy folds
　　Drooped in the breathless breeze:
As o'er a field of marigolds
　　Our eyes swam o'er the seas;
While here the eddies lisped and purled
　　Around the island's rim,
And up from out the underworld
　　We saw the mermen swim.

And it was dawn and middle-day
　　And midnight—for the moon
On silver rounds across the bay
　　Had climbed the skies of June,—

707

And there the glowing, glorious king
  Of day ruled o'er his realm,
With stars of midnight glittering
  About his diadem.

The sea-gull reeled on languid wing
  In circles round the mast,
We heard the songs the sirens sing
  As we went sailing past;
And up and down the golden sands
  A thousand fairy throngs
Flung at us from their flashing hands
  The echoes of their songs.

O it was but a dream I had
  While the musician played!—
For here the sky, and here the glad
  Old ocean kissed the glade;
And here the laughing ripples ran,
  And here the roses grew
That threw a kiss to every man
  That voyaged with the crew.

FAITH

THE sea was breaking at my feet,
  And looking out across the tide,
Where placid waves and heaven meet,
  I thought me of the Other Side.

For on the beach on which I stood
  Were wastes of sands, and wash, and roar,
Low clouds, and gloom, and solitude,
  And wrecks, and ruins—nothing more.

"O, tell me if beyond the sea
  A heavenly port there is!" I cried,
And back the echoes laughingly
  "There is! there is!" replied.

BE OUR FORTUNES AS THEY MAY

BE our fortunes as they may,
  Touched with loss or sorrow,
Saddest eyes that weep to-day
  May be glad to-morrow.

Yesterday the rain was here,
  And the winds were blowing—
Sky and earth and atmosphere
  Brimmed and overflowing.

But to-day the sun is out,
  And the drear November
We were then so vexed about
  Now we scarce remember.

Yesterday you lost a friend—
  Bless your heart and love it!—
For you scarce could comprehend
  All the aching of it;—

But I sing to you and say:
  Let the lost friend sorrow—
Here's another come to-day,
  Others may to-morrow.

A HINT OF SPRING

'TWAS but a hint of Spring—for still
    The atmosphere was sharp and chill,
Save where the genial sunshine smote
The shoulders of my overcoat,
And o'er the snow beneath my feet
Laid spectral fences down the street.

My *shadow,* even, seemed to be
Elate with some new buoyancy,
And bowed and bobbed in my advance
With trippingest extravagance,
And, when the birds chirpt out somewhere,
It seemed to wheel with me and stare.

Above I heard a rasping stir—
And on a roof the carpenter
Was perched, and prodding rusty leaves
From out the choked and dripping eaves—
And some one, hammering about,
Was taking all the windows out.

Old scraps of shingles fell before
The noisy mansion's open door;
And wrangling children raked the yard,
And labored much, and laughed as hard,
And fired the burning trash I smelt
And sniffed again—so good I felt!

LAST NIGHT—AND THIS

LAST night—how deep the darkness was!
    And well I knew its depths, because
I waded it from shore to shore,
Thinking to reach the light no more.

She would not even touch my hand.—
The winds rose and the cedars fanned
The moon out, and the stars fled back
In heaven and hid—and all was black!

But ah! To-night a summons came,
Signed with a tear-drop for a name,—
For as I wondering kissed it, lo,
A line beneath it told me so.

And *now*—the moon hangs over me
A disk of dazzling brilliancy,
And every star-tip stabs my sight
With splintered glitterings of light!

LITTLE GIRLY-GIRL

LITTLE Girly-Girl, of you
    Still forever I am dreaming.—
Laughing eyes of limpid blue—
    Tresses glimmering and gleaming
Like glad waters running over
Shelving shallows, rimmed with clover,
    Trembling where the eddies whirl,
    Gurgling, "Little Girly-Girl!"

For your name it came to me
    Down the brink of brooks that brought it
Out of Paradise—and we—
    Love and I—we, leaning, caught it
From the ripples romping nigh us,
And the bubbles bumping by us
    Over shoals of pebbled pearl,
    Lilting, "Little Girly-Girl!"

That was long and long ago,
    But in memory the tender
Winds of summer weather blow,
    And the roses burst in splendor;
And the meadow's grassy billows
Break in blossoms round the willows
    Where the currents curve and curl,
    Calling, "Little Girly-Girl!"

CLOSE THE BOOK

CLOSE the book, and leave the tale
    All unfinished. It is best:
Brighter fancy will not fail
    To relate the rest.

We have read it on and on,
    Till each character, in sooth,
By the master-touches drawn,
    Is a living truth.

Leave it so, and let us sit,
    With the volume laid away—
Cut no other leaf of it,
    But as Fancy may.—

Then the friends that we have met
    In its pages will endure,
And the villain, even yet,
    May be white and pure.

Close the book, and leave the tale
    All unfinished. It is best:
Brighter fancy will not fail
    To relate the rest.

THE MOTHER SAINTED

FAIR girl, fond wife, and dear
    Young mother, sleeping here
        So quietly,—
Tell us what dream is thine—
What miracle divine
        Is wrought in thee!

Once—was it yesterday,
Or but one hour away?—
        The folded hands
Were quick to greet our own—
Now—are they God's alone?
        Who understands?

Who, bending low to fold
The fingers as of old
        In pressure warm,
But muses,—"Surely she
Will reach one touch to me,
        And break the charm!"

And yet she does not stir;—
Such silence lies on her
        We hear the drip

Of tear-drops as we press
Our kisses answerless
   On brow and lip.

Not e'en the yearning touch
Of lips she loved so much
   She made their breath
One with her own, will she
Give answer to and be
   Wooed back from death.

And though he kneel and plead
Who was her greatest need,
   And on her cheek
Lay the soft baby-face
In its old resting-place,
   She will not speak.

So brave she was, and good—
In worth of womanhood
   So like the snow—
She, smiling, gave her life
To blend the name of wife
   With mother.—So,

God sees in her a worth
Too great for this dull earth,
   And, beckoning, stands
At Heaven's open gate
Where all His angels wait
   With welcoming hands.

Then, like her, reconciled,
O parent, husband, child,
    And mourning friend,—
Smile out as smiles the light
Of day above the night,
    And—wait the end.

THE LOST THRILL

I GROW so weary, someway, of all things
 That love and loving have vouchsafed to
  me,
 Since now all dreamed-of sweets of ecstacy
Am I possessed of: The caress that clings—
The lips that mix with mine with murmurings
 No language may interpret, and the free,
 Unfettered brood of kisses, hungrily
Feasting in swarms on honeyed blossomings
Of passion's fullest flower—For yet I miss
 The essence that alone makes love divine—
The subtle flavoring no tang of this
 Weak wine of melody may here define :—
A something found and lost in the first kiss
 A lover ever poured through lips of mine.

REACH YOUR HAND TO ME

REACH your hand to me, my friend,
  With its heartiest caress—
Sometime there will come an end
  To its present faithfulness—
    Sometime I may ask in vain
    For the touch of it again,
    When between us land or sea
    Holds it ever back from me.

Sometime I may need it so,
  Groping somewhere in the night,
It will seem to me as though
  Just a touch, however light,
    Would make all the darkness day,
    And along some sunny way
    Lead me through an April-shower
    Of my tears to this fair hour.

O the present is too sweet
  To go on forever thus!
Round the corner of the street
  Who can say what waits for us?—
    Meeting—greeting, night and day,
    Faring each the selfsame way—
    Still somewhere the path must end—
    Reach your hand to me, my friend!

719

WE MUST GET HOME

WE must get home! How could we stray like
    this?—
So far from home, we know not where it is,—
Only in some fair, apple-blossomy place
Of children's faces—and the mother's face—
We dimly dream it, till the vision clears
Even in the eyes of fancy, glad with tears.

We must get home—for we have been away
So long, it seems forever and a day!
And O so very homesick we have grown,
The laughter of the world is like a moan
In our tired hearing, and its song as vain,—
We must get home—we must get home again!

We must get home! With heart and soul we yearn
To find the long-lost pathway, and return! . . .
The child's shout lifted from the questing band
Of old folk, faring weary, hand in hand,
But faces brightening, as if clouds at last
Were showering sunshine on us as they passed.

We must get home: It hurts so, staying here,
Where fond hearts must be wept out tear by tear,
And where to wear wet lashes means, at best,
When most our lack, the least our hope of rest—
When most our need of joy, the more our pain—
We must get home—we must get home again!

We must get home—home to the simple things—
The morning-glories twirling up the strings
And bugling color, as they blared in blue-
And-white o'er garden-gates we scampered through;
The long grape-arbor, with its under-shade
Blue as the green and purple overlaid.

We must get home: All is so quiet there:
The touch of loving hands on brow and hair—
Dim rooms, wherein the sunshine is made mild—
The lost love of the mother and the child
Restored in restful lullabies of rain,—
We must get home—we must get home again!

The rows of sweetcorn and the China beans
Beyond the lettuce-beds where, towering, leans
The giant sunflower in barbaric pride
Guarding the barn-door and the lane outside;
The honeysuckles, midst the hollyhocks,
That clamber almost to the martin-box.

We must get home, where, as we nod and drowse,
Time humors us and tiptoes through the house,
And loves us best when sleeping baby-wise,
With dreams—not tear-drops—brimming our
    clenched eyes,—
Pure dreams that know nor taint nor earthly
    stain—
We must get home—we must get home again!

We must get home! There only may we find
The little playmates that we left behind,—
Some racing down the road; some by the brook;
Some droning at their desks, with wistful look
Across the fields and orchards—farther still
Where laughs and weeps the old wheel at the mill.

We must get home! The willow-whistle's call
Trills crisp and liquid as the waterfall—
Mocking the trillers in the cherry-trees
And making discord of such rhymes as these,
That know nor lilt nor cadence but the birds
First warbled—then all poets afterwards.

We must get home; and, unremembering there
All gain of all ambition otherwhere,
Rest—from the feverish victory, and the crown
Of conquest whose waste glory weighs us down.—
Fame's fairest gifts we toss back with disdain—
We must get home—we must get home again!

We must get home again—we must—we must!—
(Our rainy faces pelted in the dust)
Creep back from the vain quest through endless
    strife
To find not anywhere in all of life
A happier happiness than blest us then. . . .
We must get home—we must get home again!

MABEL

SWEET little face, so full of slumber now—
    Sweet lips unlifted now with any kiss—
Sweet dimpled cheek and chin, and snowy brow,—
        What quietude is this?

O speak! Have you forgotten, yesterday,
    How gladly you came running to the gate
To meet us in the old familiar way,
        So joyous—so elate—

So filled with wildest glee, yet so serene
    With innocence of song and childish chat,
With all the dear caresses in between—
        Have you forgotten that?

Have you forgotten, knowing gentler charms,
    The boisterous love of one you ran to greet
When you last met, who caught you in his arms
        And kissed you, in the street?

Not very many days have passed since then,
    And yet between that kiss and him there lies
No pathway of return—unless again,
        In streets of Paradise,

Your eager feet come twinkling down the gold
  Of some bright thoroughfare ethereal,
To meet and greet him there just as of old.—
    Till then, farewell—farewell.

AT DUSK

A SOMETHING quiet and subdued
 In all the faces that we meet;
A sense of rest, a solitude
 O'er all the crowded street;
  The very noises seem to be
  Crude utterings of harmony,
  And all we hear, and all we see,
 Has in it something sweet.

Thoughts come to us as from a dream
 Of some long-vanished yesterday;
The voices of the children seem
 Like ours, when young as they;
  The hand of Charity extends
  To meet Misfortune's, where it blends,
  Veiled by the dusk—and oh, my friends,
 Would it were dusk alway!

ANOTHER RIDE FROM GHENT TO AIX

WE sprang for the side-holts—my gripsack
    and I—
It dangled—I dangled—we both dangled by.
"Good speed!" cried mine host, as we landed at
    last—
"Speed?" chuckled the watch we went lumbering
    past;
Behind shut the switch, and out through the rear
    door
I glared while we waited a half hour more.

I had missed the express that went thundering
    down
Ten minutes before to my next lecture town,
And my only hope left was to catch this "wild
    freight,"
Which the landlord remarked was "most luckily
    late—
But the twenty miles distance was easily done,
If they run half as fast as they usually run!"

Not a word to each other—we struck a snail's
    pace—
Conductor and brakeman ne'er changing a place—
Save at the next watering-tank, where they all

Got out—strolled about—cut their names on the
      wall,
Or listlessly loitered on down to the pile
Of sawed wood just beyond us, to doze for a while.

'Twas high noon at starting, but while we drew
      near
"Arcady" I said, "We'll not make it, I fear!
I must strike Aix by eight, and it's three o'clock
      now;
Let me stoke up that engine, and I'll show you
      how!"
At which the conductor, with patience sublime,
Smiled up from his novel with, "Plenty of time!"

At "Trask," as we jolted stock-still as a stone,
I heard a cow bawl in a five o'clock tone;
And the steam from the saw-mill looked misty and
      thin,
And the snarl of the saw had been stifled within:
And a frowzy-haired boy, with a hat full of chips,
Came out and stared up with a smile on his lips.

At "Booneville," I groaned, "Can't I telegraph on?"
No! Why? " 'Cause the telegraph-man had just
      gone
To visit his folks in Almo"—and one heard
The sharp snap of my teeth through the throat of a
      word,
That I dragged for a mile and a half up the track,
And strangled it there, and came skulkingly back.

Again we were off. It was twilight, and more,
As we rolled o'er a bridge where beneath us the
  roar
Of a river came up with so wooing an air
I mechanic'ly strapped myself fast in my chair
As a brakeman slid open the door for more light,
Saying: "Captain, brace up, for your town is in
  sight!"

"How they'll greet me!"—and all in a moment—
  "che-wang!"
And the train stopped again, with a bump and a
  bang.
What was it? "The section-hands, just in ad-
  vance."
And I spit on my hands, and I rolled up my pants,
And I clumb like an imp that the fiends had let loose
Up out of the depths of that deadly caboose.

I ran the train's length—I lept safe to the ground—
And the legend still lives that for five miles around
They heard my voice hailing the hand-car that
  yanked
Me aboard at my bidding, and gallantly cranked,
As I groveled and clung, with my eyes in eclipse,
And a rim of red foam round my rapturous lips.

Then I cast loose my ulster—each ear-tab let fall—
Kicked off both my shoes—let go arctics and all—
Stood up with the boys—leaned—patted each head

As it bobbed up and down with the speed that we
  sped;
Clapped my hands—laughed and sang—any noise,
  bad or good,
Till at length into Aix we rotated and stood.

And all I remember is friends flocking round
As I unsheathed my head from a hole in the
  ground;
And no voice but was praising that hand-car divine,
As I rubbed down its spokes with that lecture of
  mine,
Which (the citizens voted by common consent)
Was no more than its due. 'Twas the lecture they
  meant.

THE RIPEST PEACH

THE ripest peach is highest on the tree—
　And so her love, beyond the reach of me,
Is dearest in my sight.　Sweet breezes, bow
Her heart down to me where I worship now!

She looms aloft where every eye may see
The ripest peach is highest on the tree.
Such fruitage as her love I know, alas!
I may not reach here from the orchard grass.

I drink the sunshine showered past her lips
As roses drain the dewdrop as it drips.
The ripest peach is highest on the tree,
And so mine eyes gaze upward eagerly.

Why—why do I not turn away in wrath
And pluck some heart here hanging in my path?—
Love's lower boughs bend with them—but, ah me!
The ripest peach is highest on the tree!

BEDOUIN

O LOVE is like an untamed steed!—
  So hot of heart and wild of speed,
And with fierce freedom so in love,
The desert is not vast enough,
With all its leagues of glimmering sands,
To pasture it! Ah, that my hands
Were more than human in their strength,
That my deft lariat at length
Might safely noose this splendid thing
That so defies all conquering!
Ho! but to see it whirl and reel—
The sands spurt forward—and to feel
The quivering tension of the thong
That throned me high, with shriek and song!
To grapple tufts of tossing mane—
To spurn it to its feet again,
And then, sans saddle, rein or bit,
To lash the mad life out of it!

A DITTY OF NO TONE—

Piped to the Spirit of John Keats

I

WOULD that my lips might pour out in thy
      praise
  A fitting melody—an air sublime,—
A song sun-washed and draped in dreamy haze—
  The floss and velvet of luxurious rhyme:
A lay wrought of warm languors, and o'er-brimmed
  With balminess, and fragrance of wild flowers
    Such as the droning bee ne'er wearies of—
Such thoughts as might be hymned
  To thee from this midsummer land of ours
    Through shower and sunshine, blent for very
      love.

II

Deep silences in woody aisles wherethrough
  Cool paths go loitering, and where the trill
Of best-remembered birds hath something new
  In cadence for the hearing—lingering still

Through all the open day that lies beyond;
  Reaches of pasture-lands, vine-wreathen oaks,
    Majestic still in pathos of decay;—
The road—the wayside pond
  Wherein the dragon-fly an instant soaks
    His filmy wing-tips ere he flits away.

III

And I would pluck from out the dank, rich mold,
  Thick-shaded from the sun of noon, the long
Lithe stalks of barley, topped with ruddy gold,
  And braid them in the meshes of my song;
And with them I would tangle wheat and rye,
  And wisps of greenest grass the katydid
    E'er crept beneath the blades of, sulkily,
As harvest-hands went by;
  And weave of all, as wildest fancy bid,
    A crown of mingled song and bloom for thee.

THE SPHINX

I KNOW all about the Sphinx—
  I know even what she thinks,
Staring with her stony eyes
Up forever at the skies.

For last night I dreamed that she
Told me all the mystery—
Why for æons mute she sat:—
She was just cut out for that!

MOTHER GOOSE

DEAR Mother Goose! most motherly and
  dear
 Of all good mothers who have laps wherein
 We children nestle safest from all sin,—
I cuddle to thy bosom, with no fear
There to confess that though thy cap be queer,
 And thy curls gimlety, and thy cheeks thin,
 And though the winkered mole upon thy chin
Tickles thy very nose-tip,—still to hear
 The jolly jingles of mine infancy
Crooned by thee, makes mine eager arms, as now,
 To twine about thy neck, full tenderly
Drawing the dear old face down, that thy brow
 May dip into my purest kiss, and be
 Crowned ever with the baby-love of me.

IN THE HEART OF JUNE

IN the heart of June, love,
  You and I together,
On from dawn till noon, love,
  Laughing with the weather;
Blending both our souls, love,
  In the selfsame tune,
Drinking all life holds, love,
  In the heart of June.

In the heart of June, love,
  With its golden weather,
Underneath the moon, love,
  You and I together.
Ah! how sweet to seem, love,
  Drugged and half aswoon
With this luscious dream, love,
  In the heart of June.

MY BOY

YOU smile and you smoke your cigar,
    my boy;
  You walk with a languid swing;
You tinkle and tune your guitar, my boy,
  And lift up your voice and sing;
The midnight moon is a friend of yours,
  And a serenade your joy—
And it's only an age like mine that cures
  A trouble like yours, my boy!

THE ASSASSIN

FLING him amongst the cobbles of the street
   Midmost along a mob's most turbid tide;
  Stun him with tumult upon every side—
Wrangling of hoarsened voices that repeat
His awful guilt and howl for vengeance meet;
  Let white-faced women stare, all torrid-eyed,
   With hair blown forward, and with jaws dropped
      wide,
And some face like his mother's glimmer sweet
An instant in the hot core of his eyes.
   Then snatch him with claw hands, and thong his
      head
That he may look no way but toward the skies
   That glower lividly and crackle red,—
There let some knuckled fist of lightning rise—
   Draw backward flickeringly and knock him dead.

BECAUSE

WHY did we meet long years of yore?
    And why did we strike hands and
      say:
"We will be friends, and nothing more";
    Why are we musing thus to-day?
      Because because was just because,
      And no one knew just why it was.

Why did I say good-by to you?
    Why did I sail across the main?
Why did I love not heaven's own blue
    Until I touched these shores again?
      Because because was just because,
      And you nor I knew why it was.

Why are my arms about you now,
    And happy tears upon your cheek?
And why my kisses on your brow?
    Look up in thankfulness and speak!
      Because because was just because,
      And only God knew why it was.

PANSIES

PANSIES! Pansies! How I love you, pansies!
  Jaunty-faced, laughing-lipped and dewy-eyed
    with glee;
Would my song but blossom out in little five-leaf
    stanzas
          As delicate in fancies
            As your beauty is to me!

But my eyes shall smile on you, and my hands
    infold you,
  Pet, caress, and lift you to the lips that love
      you so,
That, shut ever in the years that may mildew or
    mold you,
          My fancy shall behold you
            Fair as in the long ago.

Beautiful little blossoms
how I love you,

BABY'S DYING

BABY'S dying,
  Do not stir—
    Let her spirit lightly float
Through the sighing
  Lips of her—
    Still the murmur in the throat;
    Let the moan of grief be curbed—
    Baby must not be disturbed!

Baby's dying,
  Do not stir—
    Let her pure life lightly swim
Through the sighing
  Lips of her—
    Out from us and up to HIM—
    Let her leave us with that smile—
    Kiss and miss her after while.

AN EMPTY GLOVE

I

AN empty glove—long withering in the grasp
Of Time's cold palm. I lift it to my lips,—
And lo, once more I thrill beneath its clasp,
  In fancy, as with odorous finger-tips
    It reaches from the years that used to be
    And proffers back love, life and all, to me.

II

Ah! beautiful she was beyond belief:
  Her face was fair and lustrous as the moon's;
Her eyes—too large for small delight or grief,—
  The smiles of them were Laughter's afternoons;
    Their tears were April showers, and their
        love—
    All sweetest speech swoons ere it speaks
        thereof.

III

White-fruited cocoa shown against the shell
  Were not so white as was her brow below
The cloven tresses of the hair that fell

Across her neck and shoulders of nude snow;
  Her cheeks—chaste pallor, with a crimson
      stain—
  Her mouth was like a red rose rinsed with rain.

IV

And this was she my fancy held as good—
  As fair and lovable—in every wise
As peerless in pure worth of womanhood
  As was her wondrous beauty in men's eyes.—
    Yet, all alone, I kiss this empty glove—
    The poor husk of the hand I loved—and love.

TO THE CRICKET

THE chiming seas may clang; and Tubal Cain
  May clink his tinkling metals as he may;
  Or Pan may sit and pipe his breath away;
Or Orpheus wake his most entrancing strain
Till not a note of melody remain!—
    But thou, O cricket, with thy roundelay,
    Shalt laugh them all to scorn! So wilt thou,
        pray
Trill me thy glad song o'er and o'er again:
  I shall not weary; there is purest worth
In thy sweet prattle, since it sings the lone
  Heart home again. Thy warbling hath no
       dearth
Of childish memories—no harsher tone
  Than we might listen to in gentlest mirth,
  Thou poor plebeian minstrel of the hearth.

THE OLD-FASHIONED BIBLE

HOW dear to my heart are the scenes of my
        childhood
    That now but in mem'ry I sadly review;
The old meeting-house at the edge of the wildwood,
    The rail fence and horses all tethered thereto;
The low, sloping roof, and the bell in the steeple,
    The doves that came fluttering out overhead
As it solemnly gathered the God-fearing people
    To hear the old Bible my grandfather read.
            The old-fashioned Bible—
                The dust-covered Bible—
    The leathern-bound Bible my grandfather read.

The blessed old volume! The face bent above it—
    As now I recall it—is gravely severe,
Though the reverent eye that droops downward to
        love it
    Makes grander the text through the lens of a tear,
And, as down his features it trickles and glistens,
    The cough of the deacon is stilled, and his head
Like a haloéd patriarch's leans as he listens
    To hear the old Bible my grandfather read.
            The old-fashioned Bible—
                The dust-covered Bible—
    The leathern-bound Bible my grandfather read.

Ah! who shall look backward with scorn and
      derision
  And scoff the old book though it uselessly lies
In the dust of the past, while this newer revision
  Lisps on of a hope and a home in the skies?
Shall the voice of the Master be stifled and riven?
  Shall we hear but a tithe of the words He has said,
When so long He has, listening, leaned out of
      Heaven
To hear the old Bible my grandfather read?
      The old-fashioned Bible—
        The dust-covered Bible—
The leathern-bound Bible my grandfather read.

THE LAND OF USED-TO-BE

AND where's the Land of Used-to-be, does little
baby wonder?
Oh, we will clap a magic saddle over "Poppie's"
knee
And ride away around the world, and in and out
and under
The whole of all the golden sunny Summer-time
and see.

Leisurely and lazy-like we'll jostle on our journey,
And let the pony bathe his hooves and cool them
in the dew,
As he sidles down the shady way, and lags along the
ferny
And green, grassy edges of the lane we travel
through.

And then we'll canter on to catch the bauble of the
thistle
As it bumps among the butterflies and glimmers
down the sun,

To leave us laughing, all content to hear the robin
      whistle
  Or guess what Katydid is saying little Katy's
     done.

And pausing here a minute, where we hear the
      squirrel chuckle
  As he darts from out the underbrush and
     scampers up the tree,
We will gather buds and locust-blossoms, leaves and
      honeysuckle,
  To wreathe around our foreheads, riding into
     Used-to-be;—

For here's the very rim of it that we go swinging
      over—
  Don't you hear the Fairy bugles, and the tinkle
     of the bells,
And see the baby-bumblebees that tumble in the
      clover
  And dangle from the tilted pinks and tipsy pim-
     pernels?

And don't you see the merry faces of the daffo-
      dillies,
  And the jolly Johnny-jump-ups, and the butter-
     cups a-glee,
And the low, lolling ripples ring around the water-
      lilies?—
  All greeting us with laughter, to the Land of
     Used-to-be!

And here among the blossoms of the blooming vines
    and grasses,
  With a haze forever hanging in the sky forever
    blue,
And with a breeze from over seas to kiss us as it
    passes,
  We will romp around forever as the airy Elfins
    do!

For all the elves of earth and air are swarming here
    together—
  The prankish Puck, King Oberon, and Queen
    Titania too;
And dear old Mother Goose herself, as sunny as the
    weather,
  Comes dancing down the dewy walks to welcome
    me and you!

JUST TO BE GOOD

JUST to be good—
        This is enough—enough!
O we who find sin's billows wild and rough,
Do we not feel how more than any gold
Would be the blameless life we led of old
While yet our lips knew but a mother's kiss!
      Ah! though we miss
      All else but this,
          To be good is enough!

It is enough—
        Enough—just to be good!
To lift our hearts where they are understood,
To let the thirst for worldly power and place
Go unappeased; to smile back in God's face
With the glad lips our mothers used to kiss.
      Ah! though we miss
      All else but this,
          To be good is enough!

A LOUNGER

HE leaned against a lamp-post, lost
   In some mysterious reverie:
His head was bowed; his arms were crossed;
   He yawned, and glanced evasively:
Uncrossed his arms, and slowly put
   Them back again, and scratched his side—
Shifted his weight from foot to foot,
   And gazed out no-ward, idle-eyed.

Grotesque of form and face and dress,
   And picturesque in every way—
   A figure that from day to day
Drooped with a limper laziness;
   A figure such as artists lean,
   In pictures where distress is seen,
Against low hovels where we guess
   No happiness has ever been.

MR. WHAT'S-HIS-NAME

THEY called him Mr. What's-his-name:
From where he was, or why he came,
Or when, or what he found to do,
Nobody in the city knew.

He lived, it seemed, shut up alone
In a low hovel of his own;
There cooked his meals and made his bed,
Careless of all his neighbors said.

His neighbors, too, said many things
Expressive of grave wonderings,
Since none of them had ever been
Within his doors, or peered therein.

In fact, grown watchful, they became
Assured that Mr. What's-his-name
Was up to something wrong—indeed,
Small doubt of it, we all agreed.

At night were heard strange noises there,
When honest people everywhere
Had long retired; and his light
Was often seen to burn all night.

He left his house but seldom—then
Would always hurry back again,
As though he feared some stranger's knock,
Finding him gone, might burst the lock.

Besides, he carried, every day,
At the one hour he went away,
A basket, with the contents hid
Beneath its woven willow lid.

And so we grew to greatly blame
This wary Mr. What's-his-name,
And look on him with such distrust
His actions seemed to sanction just.

But when he died—he died one day—
Dropped in the street while on his way
To that old wretched hut of his—
You'll think it strange—perhaps it is—

But when we lifted him, and past
The threshold of his home at last,
No man of all the crowd but stepped
With reverence,—ay, *quailed* and *wept!*

What was it? Just a shriek of pain
I pray to never hear again—
A withered woman, old and bowed,
That fell and crawled and cried aloud—

And kissed the dead man's matted hair—
Lifted his face and kissed him there—
Called to him, as she clutched his hand,
In words no one could understand.

Insane? Yes.—Well, we, searching, found
An unsigned letter, in a round
Free hand, within the dead man's breast:
"Look to my mother—*I'm* at rest.

"You'll find my money safely hid
Under the lining of the lid
Of my work-basket. It is hers,
And God will bless her ministers!"

And some day—though he died unknown—
If through the City by the Throne
I walk, all cleansed of earthly shame,
I'll ask for Mr. What's-his-name.

UNCOMFORTED

LELLOINE! Lelloine! Don't you hear me
     calling?
  Calling through the night for you, and calling
    through the day;
Calling when the dawn is here, and when the dusk
  is falling—
  Calling for my Lelloine the angels lured away!

Lelloine! I call and listen, starting from my
     pillow—
  In the hush of midnight, Lelloine! I cry,
And o'er the rainy window-pane I hear the weeping
  willow
  Trail its dripping leaves like baby-fingers in reply.

Lelloine, I miss the glimmer of your glossy tresses,
  I miss the dainty velvet palms that nestled in my
    own;
And all my mother-soul went out in answerless
  caresses,
  And a storm of tears and kisses when you left me
  here alone.

I have prayed, O Lelloine, but Heaven will not hear
     me,
   I can not gain one sign from Him who leads you
     by the hand;
And O it seems that ne'er again His mercy will
     come near me—
   That He will never see my need, nor ever
     understand.

Won't you listen, Lelloine?—just a little leaning
   O'er the walls of Paradise—lean and hear my
     prayer,
And interpret death to Him in all its awful meaning,
   And tell Him you are lonely without your mother
     there.

MY WHITE BREAD

DEM good old days done past and gone
In old Ca'line wha I wuz bo'n
W'en my old Misst'ess she fust sayd,
"Yo's a-eatin' yo' white braid!"
Oh, dem's de times uts done gone by
W'en de nights shine cla, an' de coon clim'
high,
An' I sop my soul in 'possum-pie,
Das a-eatin' my white braid!

It's dem's de nights ut I cross my legs
An' pat de flo' ez I twis' de pegs
O' de banjo up twil de gals all sayd,
"Yo's a-eatin' yo' white braid!"
Oh, dem's de times ut I usen fo' to blow
On de long reeds cut in de old by-o,
An' de frogs jine in like dey glad fo' to know
I's a-eatin' my white braid.

An' I shet my eyes fo' to conjuh up
Dem good ole days ut fills my cup
Wid de times ut fust ole Misst'ess sayd,
"Yo's a-eatin' yo' white braid!"

Oh, dem's de dreams ut I fines de best;
An' bald an' gray ez a hornet's nest,
I drap my head on de good Lord's breast,
    Says a-eatin' my white braid!

HE AND I

JUST drifting on together—
    He and I—
As through the balmy weather
    Of July
  Drift two thistle-tufts embedded
  Each in each—by zephyrs wedded—
  Touring upward, giddy-headed,
    For the sky.

And, veering up and onward,
    Do we seem
Forever drifting dawnward
    In a dream,
  Where we meet song-birds that know us,
  And the winds their kisses blow us,
  While the years flow far below us
    Like a stream.

And we are happy—very—
    He and I—
Aye, even glad and merry
    Though on high

"Just drifting on together—
He and I—"

The heavens are sometimes shrouded
By the midnight storm, and clouded
Till the pallid moon is crowded
    From the sky.

My spirit ne'er expresses
    Any choice
But to clothe him with caresses
    And rejoice;
  And as he laughs, it is in
  Such a tone the moonbeams glisten
  And the stars come out to listen
    To his voice.

And so, whate'er the weather,
    He and I,—
With our lives linked thus together,
    Float and fly
  As two thistle-tufts embedded
  Each in each—by zephyrs wedded—
  Touring upward, giddy-headed,
    For the sky.

FROM A BALLOON

HO! we are loose. Hear how they shout,
     And how their clamor dwindles out
Beneath us to the merest hum
Of earthly acclamation. Come,
Lean with me here and look below—
Why, bless you, man! don't tremble so!
There is no need of fear up here—
Not higher than the buzzard swings
About upon the atmosphere,
With drowsy eyes and open wings!
There, steady, now, and feast your eyes;—
See, we are tranced—we do not rise;
It is the earth that sinks from us:
But when I first beheld it thus,
And felt the breezes downward flow,
And heard all noises fail and die,
Until but silence and the sky
Above, around me, and below,—
Why, like you now, I swooned almost,
With mingled awe and fear and glee—
As giddy as an hour-old ghost
That stares into eternity.

A TWINTORETTE

HO! my little maiden
    With the glossy tresses,
  Come thou and dance with me
    A measure all divine;
Let my breast be laden
    With but thy caresses—
  Come thou and glancingly
    Mate thy face with mine.

Thou shalt trill a rondel,
    While my lips are purling
  Some dainty twitterings
    Sweeter than the birds';
And, with arms that fondle
    Each as we go twirling,
  We will kiss, with twitterings,
    Lisps and loving words.

WHAT THEY SAID

WHISPERING to themselves apart,
   They who knew her said of her,
"Dying of a broken heart—
   Death her only comforter—
      For the man she loved is dead—
      She will follow soon!" they said.

Beautiful? Ah! brush the dust
   From Raphael's fairest face,
And restore it, as it must
   First have smiled back from its place
      On his easel as he leant
      Wrapt in awe and wonderment!

Why, to kiss the very hem
   Of the mourning-weeds she wore,
Like the winds that rustled them,
   I had gone the round world o'er;
      And to touch her hand I swear
      All things dareless I would dare!

But unto themselves apart,
  Whispering, they said of her,
"Dying of a broken heart—
  Death her only comforter—
    For the man she loved is dead—
    She will follow soon!" they said.

So I mutely turned away,
  Turned with sorrow and despair,
Yearning still from day to day
  For that woman dying there,
    Till at last, by longing led,
    I returned to find her—dead?

"Dead?"—I know that word would tell
  Rhyming there—but in this case
"Wed" rhymes equally as well
  In the very selfsame place—
    And, in fact, the latter word
    Is the one she had preferred.

Yet unto themselves apart,
  Whisp'ring they had said of her—
"Dying of a broken heart—
  Death her only comforter—
    For the man she loved is dead—
    She will follow soon!" they said.

AFTER THE FROST

AFTER the frost! O the rose is dead,
And the weeds lie pied in the garden-bed,
And the peach tree's shade in the wan sunshine.
Faint as the veins in these hands of mine,
Streaks the gray of the orchard wall
Where the vine rasps loose, and the last leaves
fall,
And the bare boughs writhe, and the winds are
lost—
After the frost—the frost!

After the frost! O the weary head
And the hands and the heart are quietéd;
And the lips we loved are locked at last,
And kiss not back, though the rain falls fast
And the lashes drip, and the soul makes moan,
And on through the dead leaves walks alone
Where the bare boughs writhe and the winds are
lost—
After the frost—the frost!

CHARLES H. PHILIPS

OBIT NOVEMBER 5TH, 1881

O FRIEND! There is no way
   To bid farewell to thee!
The words that we would say
Above thy grave to-day
Still falter and delay
   And fail us utterly.

When walking with us here,
   The hand we loved to press
Was gentle, and sincere
As thy frank eyes were clear
Through every smile and tear
   Of pleasure and distress.

In years, young; yet in thought
   Mature; thy spirit, free,
And fired with fervor caught
Of thy proud sire, who fought
His way to fame, and taught
   Its toilsome way to thee.

So even thou hast gained
   The victory God-given—
Yea, as our cheeks are stained
With tears, and our souls pained
And mute, thou hast attained
   Thy high reward in Heaven!

WHEN IT RAINS

WHEN it rains, and with the rain
    Never bird has heart to sing,
And across the window-pane
  Is no sunlight glimmering;
When the pitiless refrain
  Brings a tremor to the lips,
Our tears are like the rain
  As it drips, drips, drips—
  Like the sad, unceasing rain as it drips.

When the light of heaven's blue
  Is blurred and blotted quite,
And the dreary day to you
  Is but a long twilight;
When it seems that ne'er again
  Shall the sun break its eclipse,
Our tears are like the rain
  As it drips, drips, drips—
  Like the endless, friendless rain as it drips.

When it rains! weary heart,
   O be of better cheer!
The leaden clouds will part,
   And the morrow will be clear;
Take up your load again,
   With a prayer upon your lips,
Thanking Heaven for the rain
   As it drips, drips, drips—
   With the golden bow of promise as it
      drips.

AN ASSASSIN

CAT LIKE he creeps along where ways are
    dim,
  From covert unto covert's secrecy;
His shadow in the moonlight shrinks from him
    And crouches warily.

He hugs strange envies to his breast, and nurses
  Wild hatreds, till the murderous hand he grips
Falls, quivering with the tension of the curses
    He launches from his lips.

Drenched in his victim's blood he holds high
    revel;
  He mocks at justice, and in all men's eyes
Insults his God—and no one but the devil
    Is sorry when he dies.

BEST OF ALL

OF all good gifts that the Lord lets fall,
Is not silence the best of all?

The deep, sweet hush when the song is closed,
And every sound but a voiceless ghost;

And every sigh, as we listening leant,
A breathless quiet of vast content?

The laughs we laughed have a purer ring
With but their memory echoing;

And the joys we voiced, and the words we said,
Seem so dearer for being dead.

So of all good gifts that the Lord lets fall,
Is not silence the best of all?

MR. SILBERBERG

I LIKE me yet dot leedle chile
  Vich climb my lap up in to-day,
  Unt took my cheap cigair avay,
Unt laugh unt kiss me, purty-whvile,—
  Possescially I like dose mout'
    Vich taste his moder's like—unt so,
  Eef my cigair it gone glean out
    —Yust let it go!

Vat I caire den for *any*ding?
  Der "HERALDT" schlip out fon my handt
  Unt all my odvairtizement standt
Mitout new changements boddering;
  I only t'ink—I haf me dis
    One leedle boy to pet unt love
  Unt play me vit, unt hug unt kiss—
    Unt dot's enough!

Der plans unt pairposes I vear
  Out in der vorld all fades avay,
  Unt vit der beeznis of der day
I got me den no time to spare;

Der caires of trade vas caires no more—
    Dem cash accoundts dey dodge me by,
Unt vit my chile I roll der floor,
    Unt laugh unt gry!

Ach! frient! dem childens is der ones
    Dot got some happy times—you bet!—
Dot's vy ven I been growed up yet
I visht I schtill been leedle vonce!
    Unt ven dot leedle roozter tries
      Dem baby-tricks I used to do,
My mout' it vater, unt my eyes
    Dey vater too!

Unt all der summer-time unt spring
    Of childhoodt it come back to me,
    So dot it vas a dream I see
Ven I yust look at anyding!
    Unt ven dot leedle boy run' by,
      I t'ink "Dot's *me,*" fon hour to hour
Schtill chasing yet dose butterfly
    Fon flower to flower!

Oxpose I vas lots money vairt,
    Vit blenty schtone-front schtore to rent,
    Unt mor'gages at twelf-per tcent.,
Unt diamondts in my ruffled shairt,—
    I make a'signment of all dot,
      Unt tairn it over vit a schmile
Aber you please—but, don'd forgot,
    I keep dot chile!

THE HEREAFTER

HEREAFTER! O we need not waste
    Our smiles or tears, whate'er
      befall:
No happiness but holds a taste
    Of something sweeter, after all;—
No depth of agony but feels
    Some fragment of abiding trust,—
Whatever Death unlocks or seals,
    The mute beyond is just.

THE LOVING CUP

TRANCED in the glamour of a dream
  Where banquet-lights and fancies gleam,
And ripest wit and wine abound,
And pledges hale go round and round,—
Lo, dazzled with enchanted rays—
As in the golden olden days
Sir Galahad—my eyes swim up
To greet your splendor, Loving Cup!

What is the secret of your art,
Linking together hand and heart
Your myriad votaries who do
Themselves most honor honoring you?
What gracious service have you done
To win the name that you have won?—
Kissing it back from tuneful lips
That sing your praise between the sips!

Your spicy breath, O Loving Cup,
That, like an incense steaming up,
Full-freighted with a fragrance fine
As ever swooned on sense of mine,

Is rare enough.—But then, ah me!
How rarer every memory
That, rising with it, wreathes and blends
In forms and faces of my friends!

O Loving Cup! in fancy still,
I clasp their hands, and feel the thrill
Of fellowship that still endures
While lips are theirs and wine is yours!
And while my memory journeys down
The years that lead to Boston Town,
Abide where first were rendered up
Our mutual loves, O Loving Cup!

EROS

THE storm of love has burst at last
　　Full on me: All the world, before,
　Was like an alien, unknown shore
Along whose verge I laughing passed.—
　　But now—I laugh not any more,—
Bowed with a silence vast in weight
　　As that which falls on one who stands
　　For the first time on ocean sands,
Seeing and feeling all the great
　　Awe of the waves as they wash the lands
And billow and wallow and undulate.

THE QUIET LODGER

THE man that rooms next door to me:
  Two weeks ago, this very night,
He took possession quietly,
  As any other lodger might—
    But why the room next mine should so
    Attract him I was vexed to know,—
    Because his quietude, in fine,
    Was far superior to mine.

"Now, I like quiet, truth to tell,
  A tranquil life is sweet to me—
But *this*," I sneered, "suits me too well.—
  He shuts his door so noiselessly,
    And glides about so very mute,
    In each mysterious pursuit,
    His silence is oppressive, and
    Too deep for me to understand."

Sometimes, forgetting book or pen,
  I've found my head in breathless poise
Lifted, and dropped in shame again,
  Hearing some alien ghost of noise—

Some smothered sound that seemed to be
A trunk-lid dropped unguardedly,
Or the crisp writhings of some quire
Of manuscript thrust in the fire.

Then I have climbed, and closed in vain
  My transom, opening in the hall;
Or close against the window-pane
  Have pressed my fevered face,—but all
    The day or night without held not
    A sight or sound or counter-thought
    To set my mind one instant free
    Of this man's silent mastery.

And often I have paced the floor
  With muttering anger, far at night,
Hearing, and cursing, o'er and o'er,
  The muffled noises, and the light
    And tireless movements of this guest
    Whose silence raged above my rest
    Hoarser than howling storms at sea—
    The man that rooms next door to me.

But twice or thrice, upon the stair,
  I've seen his face—most strangely wan,—
Each time upon me unaware
  He came—smooth'd past me, and was
      gone.—
    So like a whisper he went by,
    I listened after, ear and eye,
    Nor could my chafing fancy tell
    The meaning of one syllable.

Last night I caught him, face to face,—
  He entering his room, and I
Glaring from mine: He paused a space
  And met my scowl all shrinkingly,
    But with full gentleness: The key
    Turned in his door—and I could see
    It tremblingly withdrawn and put
    Inside, and then—the door was shut.

Then silence. *Silence!*—why, last night
  The silence was tumultuous,
And thundered on till broad daylight;—
  O never has it stunned me thus!—
    It rolls, and moans, and mumbles yet.—
    Ah, God! how loud may silence get
    When man mocks at a brother man
    Who answers but as silence can!

The silence grew, and grew, and grew,
  Till at high noon to-day 'twas heard
Throughout the house; and men flocked
      through
  The echoing halls, with faces blurred
    With pallor, gloom, and fear, and awe,
    And shuddering at what they saw,—
    The quiet lodger, as he lay
    Stark of the life he cast away.
   .   .   .   .   .   .

So strange to-night—those voices there,
  Where all so quiet was before:
They say the face has not a care
  Nor sorrow in it any more. . . .

His latest scrawl:—"Forgive me—You
Who prayed, 'They know not what they
    do!'"
My tears will never let me see
This man that rooms next door to me!

THE BROOK-SONG

LITTLE brook! Little brook!
  You have such a happy look—
Such a very merry manner, as you swerve and curve
        and crook—
        And your ripples, one and one,
        Reach each other's hands and run
Like laughing little children in the sun!

        Little brook, sing to me:
        Sing about a bumblebee
That tumbled from a lily-bell and grumbled mumb-
        lingly,
        Because he wet the film
        Of his wings, and had to swim,
While the water-bugs raced round and laughed at
        him!

        Little brook—sing a song
        Of a leaf that sailed along
Down the golden-braided center of your current
        swift and strong,
        And a dragon-fly that lit
        On the tilting rim of it,
And rode away and wasn't scared a bit.

And sing—how oft in glee
Came a truant boy like me,
Who loved to lean and listen to your lilting melody,
Till the gurgle and refrain
Of your music in his brain
Wrought a happiness as keen to him as pain.

Little brook—laugh and leap!
Do not let the dreamer weep:
Sing him all the songs of summer till he sink in
softest sleep;
And then sing soft and low
Through his dreams of long ago—
Sing back to him the rest he used to know!

BIN A-FISHIN'

W'EN de sun's gone down, an' de moon
     is riz,
  Bin a-fishin'! Bin a-fishin'!
It's I's aguine down wha' the by-o is!
  Bin a-fishin' all night long!

CHORUS

  Bin a-fishin'! Bin a-fishin'!
Bin a-fishin' clean fum de dusk of night
Twel away 'long on in de mornin' light.

Bait my hook, un I plunk her down!
  Bin a-fishin'! Bin a-fishin'!
Un I lay dat catfish weigh five pound!
  Bin a-fishin' all night long!

CHORUS

Folks tells me ut a sucker won't bite,
  Bin a-fishin'! Bin a-fishin'!
Yit I lif' out fo' last Chuesday night,
  Bin a-fishin' all night long!

CHORUS

Little fish nibble un de big fish come;
  Bin a-fishin'! Bin a-fishin'!
"Go way, little fish! I want some!"
  Bin a-fishin' all night long!

CHORUS

Sez de bullfrog, "D-runk!" sez de ole owl
        "Whoo!"
  Bin a-fishin'! Bin a-fishin'!
'Spec, Mr. Nigger, dey's a-meanin' you,
  Bin a-fishin' all night long!

CHORUS

UNCLE DAN'L IN TOWN OVER SUNDAY

I CAIN'T git used to city ways—
  Ner never could, I' bet my hat!
Jevver know jes' whur I was raised?—
Raised on a farm! D' ever tell you that?
Was undoubtatly, I declare!
And now, on Sunday—fun to spare
Around a farm! Why jes' to set
Up on the top three-cornered rail
Of Pap's old place, nigh La Fayette,
I'd swap my soul off, hide and tail!
You fellers in the city here,
You don't know nothin'!—S'pose to-day,
This clatterin' Sunday, you waked up
Without no jinglin'-janglin' bells,
Ner rattlin' of the milkman's cup,
Ner any swarm of screechin' birds
Like these here English swallers—S'pose
Ut you could miss all noise like those,
And git shet o' thinkin' of 'em afterwerds,
And then, in the country, wake and hear
Nothin' but silence—wake and see
Nothin' but green woods fur and near?—
What sort o' Sunday would that be? . . .
Wisht I hed you home with me!

Now think! The laziest of all days—
To git up any time—er sleep—
Er jes' lay round and watch the haze
A-dancin' 'crost the wheat, and keep
My pipe a-goern laisurely,
And puff and whiff as pleases me—
And ef I leave a trail of smoke
Clean through the house, no one to say,
"Wah! throw that nasty thing away;
Hev some regyard fer decency!"
To walk round barefoot, if you choose;
Er saw the fiddle—er dig some bait
And go a-fishin'—er pitch hoss shoes
Out in the shade somewhurs, and wait
For dinner-time, with an appetite
Ut folks in town cain't equal quite!
To laze around the barn and poke
Fer hens' nests—er git up a match
Betwixt the boys, and watch 'em scratch
And rassle round, and sweat and swear
And quarrel to their hearts' content;
And me a-jes' a-settin' there
A-hatchin' out more devilment!
What sort o' Sunday would that be? . . .
Wisht I hed you home with me!

EMERSON

CONCORD, APRIL 27, 1882

WHAT shall we say? In quietude,
    Within his home, in dreams un-
        guessed,
He lies; the grief a nation would
    Evince must be repressed.

Nor meet is it the loud acclaim
    His countrymen would raise—that he
Has left the riches of his fame
    The whole world's legacy.

Then, prayerful, let us pause until
    We find, as grateful spirits can,
The way most worthy to fulfil
    The tribute due the man.

Think what were best in his regard
    Who voyaged life in such a cause:
Our simplest faith were best reward—
    Our silence, best applause.

YOUR VIOLIN

YOUR violin! Ah me!
　　'Twas fashioned o'er the sea,
In storied Italy—
　　What matter where?
It is its voice that sways
And thrills me as it plays
The airs of other days—
　　The days that were!

Then let your magic bow
Glide lightly to and fro.—
I close my eyes, and so,
　　In vast content,
I kiss my hand to you,
And to the tunes we knew
Of old, as well as to
　　Your instrument!

Poured out of some dim dream
Of lulling sounds that seem
Like ripples of a stream
　　Twanged lightly by

The slender, tender hands
Of weeping-willow wands
That droop where gleaming sands
    And pebbles lie.

A melody that swoons
In all the truant tunes
Long listless afternoons
    Lure from the breeze,
When woodland boughs are stirred,
And moaning doves are heard,
And laughter afterward
    Beneath the trees.

Through all the chorusing,
I hear on leaves of spring
The drip and pattering
    Of April skies,
With echoes faint and sweet
As baby-angel feet
Might wake along a street
    Of Paradise.

SOLDIERS HERE TO-DAY

I

SOLDIERS and saviors of the homes we love;
  Heroes and patriots who marched away,
And who marched back, and who marched on
    above—
    All—all are here to-day!

By the dear cause you fought for—you are here;
  At summons of bugle, and the drum
Whose palpitating syllables were ne'er
    More musical, you come!

Here—by the stars that bloom in fields of blue,
  And by the bird above with shielding wings;
And by the flag that floats out over you,
    With silken beckonings—

Ay, here beneath its folds are gathered all
  Who warred unscathed for blessings that it
    gave—
Still blessed its champion, though it but fall
    A shadow on his grave!

"Soldiers here today"

II

We greet you, Victors, as in vast array
   You gather from the scenes of strife and
      death—
From spectral fortress-walls where curls away
     The cannon's latest breath.

We greet you—from the crumbling battlements
   Where once again the old flag feels the breeze
Stroke out its tattered stripes and smooth its rents
     With rippling ecstasies.

From living tombs where every hope seemed
      lost—
   With famine quarantined by bristling guns—
The prison-pens—the guards—the "dead-line"
      crossed
     By—riddled skeletons!

From furrowed plains, sown thick with bursting
      shells—
   From mountain gorge, and toppling crags
      o'erhead—
From wards of pestilential hospitals,
     And trenches of the dead.

III

In fancy all are here. The night is o'er,
   And through dissolving mists the morning
      gleams;

And clustered round their hearths we see once
    more
    The heroes of our dreams.

Strong, tawny faces, some, and some are fair,
    And some are marked with age's latest prime,
And, seer-like, browed and aureoled with hair
    As hoar as winter-time.

The faces of fond lovers, glorified—
    The faces of the husband and the wife—
The babe's face nestled at the mother's side,
    And smiling back at life;

A bloom of happiness in every cheek—
    A thrill of tingling joy in every vein—
In every soul a rapture they will seek
    In Heaven, and find again!

IV

'Tis not a vision only—we who pay
    But the poor tribute of our praises here
Are equal sharers in the guerdon they
    Purchased at price so dear.

The angel, Peace, o'er all uplifts her hand,
    Waving the olive, and with heavenly eyes
Shedding a light of love o'er sea and land
    As sunshine from the skies—

Her figure pedestaled on Freedom's soil—
   Her sandals kissed with seas of golden grain—
Queen of a realm of joy-requited toil
    That glories in her reign.

O blessed land of labor and reward!
   O gracious Ruler, let Thy reign endure;
In pruning-hook and plough-share beat the sword,
    And reap the harvest sure!

A WINDY DAY

THE dawn was a dawn of splendor,
　　And the blue of the morning skies
Was as placid and deep and tender
　　As the blue of a baby's eyes;
The sunshine flooded the mountain,
　　And flashed over land and sea
Like the spray of a glittering fountain.—
　　But the wind—the wind—Ah me!

Like a weird invisible spirit,
　　It swooped in its airy flight;
And the earth, as the stress drew near it,
　　Quailed as in mute affright;
The grass in the green fields quivered—
　　The waves of the smitten brook
Chillily shuddered and shivered,
　　And the reeds bowed down and shook.

Like a sorrowful miserere
　　It sobbed, and it blew and blew,
Till the leaves on the trees looked weary,
　　And my prayers were weary, too;
And then, like the sunshine's glimmer
　　That failed in the awful strain,
All the hope of my eyes grew dimmer
　　In a spatter of spiteful rain.

SHADOW AND SHINE

STORMS of the winter, and deepening
    snows,
  When will you end? I said,
For the soul within me was numb with woes,
  And my heart uncomforted.
When will you cease, O dismal days?
  When will you set me free?
For the frozen world and its desolate ways
  Are all unloved of me!

I waited long, but the answer came—
  The kiss of the sunshine lay
Warm as a flame on the lips that frame
  The song in my heart to-day.
Blossoms of summer-time waved in the air,
  Glimmers of sun in the sea;
Fair thoughts followed me everywhere,
  And the world was dear to me.

THE OLD SWIMMIN'-HOLE

OH! the old swimmin'-hole! whare the crick so
    still and deep
Looked like a baby-river that was laying half asleep,
And the gurgle of the worter round the drift jest
    below
Sounded like the laugh of something we onc't ust
    to know
Before we could remember anything but the eyes
Of the angels lookin' out as we left Paradise;
But the merry days of youth is beyond our controle.
And it's hard to part ferever with the old swimmin'-
    hole.

Oh! the old swimmin'-hole! In the happy days of
    yore,
When I ust to lean above it on the old sickamore,
Oh! it showed me a face in its warm sunny tide
That gazed back at me so gay and glorified,
It made me love myself, as I leaped to caress
My shadder smilin' up at me with sich tenderness.
But them days is past and gone, and old Time's
    tuck his toll
From the old man come back to the old swimmin'-
    hole.

"But the merry days of youth is beyond our controle,
And its hard to part ferever with the old swimmin' hole"

Oh! the old swimmin'-hole! In the long, lazy days
When the humdrum of school made so many run-
    a-ways,
How plesant was the jurney down the old dusty
    lane,
Whare the tracks of our bare feet was all printed so
    plane
You could tell by the dent of the heel and the sole
They was lots o' fun on hands at the old swimmin'-
    hole.
But the lost joys is past! Let your tears in sorrow
    roll
Like the rain that ust to dapple up the old swimmin'-
    hole.

Thare the bullrushes growed, and the cattails so tall,
And the sunshine and shadder fell over it all;
And it mottled the worter with amber and gold
Tel the glad lilies rocked in the ripples that rolled;
And the snake-feeder's four gauzy wings fluttered
    by
Like the ghost of a daisy dropped out of the sky,
Or a wownded apple-blossom in the breeze's
    controle
As it cut acrost some orchurd to'rds the old
    swimmin'-hole.

Oh! the old swimmin'-hole! When I last saw the
    place,
The scenes was all changed, like the change in my
    face;

The bridge of the railroad now crosses the spot
Whare the old divin'-log lays sunk and fergot.
And I stray down the banks whare the trees ust to
    be—
But never again will theyr shade shelter me!
And I wish in my sorrow I could strip to the soul,
And dive off in my grave like the old swimmin'-hole.

THOUGHTS FER THE DISCURAGED FARMER

THE summer winds is sniffin' round the bloomin'
    locus' trees;
And the clover in the pastur is a big day fer the
    bees,
And they been a-swiggin' honey, above board and
    on the sly,
Tel they stutter in theyr buzzin' and stagger as they
    fly.
The flicker on the fence-rail 'pears to jest spit on
    his wings
And roll up his feathers, by the sassy way he sings;
And the hoss-fly is a-whettin'-up his forelegs fer
    biz,
And the off-mare is a-switchin' all of her tale they
    is.

You can hear the blackbirds jawin' as they foller up
    the plow—
Oh, theyr bound to git theyr brekfast, and theyr not
    a-carin' how;

So they quarrel in the furries, and they quarrel on
the wing—
But theyr peaceabler in pot-pies than any other
thing:
And it's when I git my shotgun drawed up in stiddy
rest,
She's as full of tribbelation as a yeller-jacket's nest;
And a few shots before dinner, when the sun's
a-shinin' right,
Seems to kindo'-sorto' sharpen up a feller's appetite!

They's been a heap o' rain, but the sun's out to-day,
And the clouds of the wet spell is all cleared away,
And the woods is all the greener, and the grass is
greener still;
It may rain again to-morry, but I don't think it will.
Some says the crops is ruined, and the corn's
drownded out,
And propha-sy the wheat will be a failure, without
doubt;
But the kind Providence that has never failed us
yet,
Will be on hands onc't more at the 'leventh hour, I
bet!

Does the medder-lark complane, as he swims high
and dry
Through the waves of the wind and the blue of the
sky?

Does the quail set up and whissel in a disappinted
    way,
Er hang his head in silunce, and sorrow all the day?
Is the chipmuck's health a-failin'?—Does he walk,
    er does he run?
Don't the buzzards ooze around up thare jest like
    they've allus done?
Is they anything the matter with the rooster's lungs
    er voice?
Ort a mortul be complanin' when dumb animals
    rejoice?

Then let us, one and all, be contentud with our lot;
The June is here this morning, and the sun is
    shining hot.
Oh! let us fill our harts up with the glory of the day,
And banish ev'ry doubt and care and sorrow fur
    away!
Whatever be our station, with Providence fer guide,
Sich fine circumstances ort to make us satisfied;
Fer the world is full of roses, and the roses full of
    dew,
And the dew is full of heavenly love that drips fer
    me and you.

A GOOD-BY

"GOOD-BY, my friend!"
    He takes her hand—
The pressures blend:
  They understand
      But vaguely why, with drooping eye,
      Each moans—"Good-by!—Good-by!"

"Dear friend, good-by!"
  O she could smile
If she might cry
  A little while!—
      She says, "I *ought* to smile—but I—
      Forgive me—*There!*—Good-by!"

"'Good-by?' Ah, no:
  I hate," says he,
"These 'good-bys' so!"
  "And *I*," says she,
      "Detest them so—why, I should *die*
      Were this a *real* 'good-by'!"

A SUMMER'S DAY

THE Summer's put the idy in
My head that I'm a boy ag'in;
And all around's so bright and gay
I want to put my team away,
And jest git out whare I can lay
And soak my hide full of the day!
But work is work, and must be done—
Yit, as I work, I have my fun,
Jest fancyin' these furries here
Is childhood's paths onc't more so dear:—
And so I walk through medder-lands,
    And country lanes, and swampy trails
Whare long bullrushes bresh my hands;
    And, tilted on the ridered rails
Of deadnin' fences, "Old Bob White"
Whissels his name in high delight,
And whirs away. I wunder still,
Whichever way a boy's feet will—
Whare trees has fell, with tangled tops
    Whare dead leaves shakes, I stop fer breth,
Heerin' the acorn as it drops—
    H'istin' my chin up still as deth,
And watchin' clos't, with upturned eyes,

The tree whare Mr. Squirrel tries
To hide hisse'f above the limb,
But lets his own tale tell on him.
I wunder on in deeper glooms—
    Git hungry, hearin' female cries
From old farmhouses, whare perfumes
    Of harvest dinners seems to rise
And ta'nt a feller, hart and brane,
With memories he can't explane.

I wunder through the underbresh,
    Whare pig-tracks, pintin' to'rds the crick,
Is picked and printed in the fresh
    Black bottom-lands, like wimmern pick
Theyr pie-crusts with a fork, some way,
When bakin' fer camp-meetin' day.

I wunder on and on and on,
Tel my gray hair and beard is gone,
And ev'ry wrinkle on my brow
Is rubbed clean out and shaddered now
With curls as brown and fare and fine
As tenderls of the wild grape-vine
That ust to climb the highest tree
To keep the ripest ones fer me.
I wunder still, and here I am
Wadin' the ford below the dam—
The worter chucklin' round my knee
    At hornet-welt and bramble-scratch,
And me a-slippin' 'crost to see
        Ef Tyner's plums is ripe, and size

The old man's wortermelon-patch,
    With juicy mouth and drouthy eyes.
Then, after sich a day of mirth
And happiness as worlds is wurth—
    So tired that Heaven seems nigh about,—
The sweetest tiredness on earth
    Is to git home and flatten out—
So tired you can't lay flat enugh,
And sorto' wish that you could spred
Out like molasses on the bed,
And jest drip off the aidges in
The dreams that never comes ag'in.

A HYMB OF FAITH

O, THOU that doth all things devise
And fashon fer the best,
He'p us who sees with mortul eyes
To overlook the rest.

They's times, of course, we grope in doubt,
And in afflictions sore;
So knock the louder, Lord, without,
And we'll unlock the door.

Make us to feel, when times looks bad
And tears in pitty melts,
Thou wast the only he'p we had
When they was nothin' else.

Death comes alike to ev'ry man
That ever was borned on earth;
Then let us do the best we can
To live fer all life's wurth.

Ef storms and tempusts dred to see
Makes black the heavens ore,
They done the same in Galilee
Two thousand years before.

But after all, the golden sun
   Poured out its floods on them
That watched and waited fer the One
   Then borned in Bethlyham.

Also, the star of holy writ
   Made noonday of the night,
Whilse other stars that looked at it
   Was envious with delight.

The sages then in wurship bowed,
   From ev'ry clime so fare;
O, sinner, think of that glad crowd
   That congergated thare!

They was content to fall in ranks
   With One that knowed the way
From good old Jurden's stormy banks
   Clean up to Jedgmunt Day.

No matter, then, how all is mixed
   In our near-sighted eyes,
All things is fer the best, and fixed
   Out straight in Paradise.

Then take things as God sends 'em here,
   And, ef we live er die,
Be more and more contenteder,
   Without a-astin' why.

O, Thou that doth all things devise
    And fashon fer the best,
He'p us who sees with mortul eyes
    To overlook the rest.

AT BROAD RIPPLE

AH, luxury! Beyond the heat
    And dust of town, with dangling feet,
Astride the rock below the dam,
In the cool shadows where the calm
Rests on the stream again, and all
Is silent save the waterfall,—
I bait my hook and cast my line,
And feel the best of life is mine.

No high ambition may I claim—
I angle not for lordly game
Of trout, or bass, or wary bream—
A black perch reaches the extreme
Of my desires; and "goggle-eyes"
Are not a thing that I despise;
A sunfish, or a "chub," or "cat"—
A "silver-side"—yea, even that!

In eloquent tranquillity
The waters lisp and talk to me.
Sometimes, far out, the surface breaks,
As some proud bass an instant shakes

His glittering armor in the sun,
And romping ripples, one by one,
Come dallying across the space
Where undulates my smiling face.

The river's story flowing by,
Forever sweet to ear and eye,
Forever tenderly begun—
Forever new and never done.
Thus lulled and sheltered in a shade
Where never feverish cares invade,
I bait my hook and cast my line,
And feel the best of life is mine.

THE COUNTRY EDITOR

A THOUGHTFUL brow and face—of
    sallow hue,
  But warm with welcome, as we find him there,
  Throned in his old misnomered "easy chair,"
Scrawling a "leader," or a book-review;
Or staring through the roof for something new
  With which to lift a wretched rival's hair,
  Or blow some petty clique in empty air
And snap the party-ligaments in two.
  A man he is deserving well of thee,—
So be compassionate—yea, pay thy dues,
  Nor pamper him with thy spring-poetry,
But haul him wood, or something he can use;
  And promptly act, nor tarry long when he
  Gnaweth his pen and glareth rabidly.

WORTERMELON TIME

OLD wortermelon time is a-comin' round ag'in,
    And they ain't no man a-livin' any tickleder'n
      me,
Fer the way I hanker after wortermelons is a sin—
    Which is the why and wharefore, as you can
      plainly see.

Oh! it's in the sandy soil wortermelons does the
      best,
    And it's thare they'll lay and waller in the sun-
      shine and the dew
Tel they wear all the green streaks clean off of theyr
      breast;
    And you bet I ain't a-findin' any fault with them;
      air you?

They ain't no better thing in the vegetable line;
    And they don't need much 'tendin', as ev'ry
      farmer knows;
And when theyr ripe and ready fer to pluck from
      the vine,
    I want to say to you theyr the best fruit that
      grows.

It's some likes the yeller-core, and some likes the
     red,
  And it's some says "The Little Californy" is the
     best;
But the sweetest slice of all I ever wedged in my
     head,
  Is the old "Edingburg Mounting-sprout," of the
     West.

You don't want no punkins nigh your wortermelon
     vines—
  'Cause, some-way-another, they'll spile your
     melons, shore;—
I've seed 'em taste like punkins, from the core to
     the rines,
  Which may be a fact you have heerd of before.

But your melons that's raised right and 'tended to
     with care,
  You can walk around amongst 'em with a parent's
     pride and joy,
And thump 'em on the heads with as fatherly a air
  As ef each one of them was your little girl er boy.

I joy in my hart jest to hear that rippin' sound
  When you split one down the back and jolt the
     halves in two,
And the friends you love the best is gethered all
     around—
  And you says unto your sweethart, "Oh, here's
     the core fer you!"

And I like to slice 'em up in big pieces fer 'em all,
  Espeshally the childern, and watch theyr high
      delight
As one by one the rines with theyr pink notches
    falls,
  And they holler fer some more, with unquenched
      appetite.

Boys takes to it natchurl, and I like to see 'em eat—
  A slice of wortermelon's like a frenchharp in
      theyr hands,
And when they "saw" it through theyr mouth sich
    music can't be beat—
  'Cause it's music both the sperit and the stummick
      understands.

Oh, they's more in wortermelons than the purty-
    colored meat,
  And the overflowin' sweetness of the worter
      squshed betwixt
The up'ard and the down'ard motions of a feller's
    teeth,
  And it's the taste of ripe old age and juicy child-
      hood mixed.

Fer I never taste a melon but my thoughts flies
    away
  To the summer-time of youth; and again I see the
      dawn,
And the fadin' afternoon of the long summer day,
  And the dusk and dew a-fallin', and the night
      a-comin' on.

And thare's the corn around us, and the lispin'
    leaves and trees,
  And the stars a-peekin' down on us as still as
    silver mice,
And us boys in the wortermelons on our hands and
    knees,
  And the new-moon hangin' ore us like a yeller-
    cored slice.

Oh! it's wortermelon time is a-comin' round ag'in,
  And they ain't no man a-livin' any tickelder'n me,
Fer the way I hanker after wortermelons is a sin—
  Which is the why and wharefore, as you can
    plainly see.

A SONG OF THE CRUISE

O THE sun and the rain, and the rain and the
    sun!
There'll be sunshine again when the tempest is
    done;
And the storm will beat back when the shining is
    past;
But in some happy haven we'll anchor at last.
        Then murmur no more,
        In lull or in roar,
But smile and be brave till the voyage is o'er.

O the rain and the sun, and the sun and the rain!
When the tempest is done, then the sunshine again;
And in rapture we'll ride through the stormiest
    gales,
For God's hand's on the helm and His breath in
    the sails.
        Then murmur no more,
        In lull or in roar,
But smile and be brave till the voyage is o'er.

MY PHILOSOFY

I AIN'T, ner don't p'tend to be,
  Much posted on philosofy;
But thare is times, when all alone,
I work out idees of my own.
And of these same thare is a few
I'd like to jest refer to you—
Pervidin' that you don't object
To listen clos't and rickollect.

I allus argy that a man
Who does about the best he can
Is plenty good enugh to suit
This lower mundane institute—
No matter ef his daily walk
Is subject fer his neghbor's talk,
And critic-minds of ev'ry whim
Jest all git up and go fer him!

I knowed a feller onc't that had
The yeller-janders mighty bad,—
And each and ev'ry friend he'd meet
Would stop and give him some receet

Fer cuorin' of 'em. But he'd say
He kindo' thought they'd go away
Without no medicin', and boast
That he'd git well without one doste.

He kep' a-yellerin' on—and they
Perdictin' that he'd die some day
Before he knowed it! Tuck his bed,
The feller did, and lost his head,
And wundered in his mind a spell—
Then rallied, and, at last, got well;
But ev'ry friend that said he'd die
Went back on him eternally!

It's natchurl enugh, I guess,
When some gits more and some gits less,
Fer them-uns on the slimmest side
To claim it ain't a fare divide;
And I've knowed some to lay and wait,
And git up soon, and set up late,
To ketch some feller they could hate
Fer goin' at a faster gait.

The signs is bad when folks commence
A-findin' fault with Providence,
And balkin' 'cause the earth don't shake
At ev'ry prancin' step they take.
No man is grate tel he can see
How less than little he would be
Ef stripped to self, and stark and bare
He hung his sign out anywhare.

My doctern is to lay aside
Contensions, and be satisfied:
Jest do your best, and praise er blame
That follers that, counts jest the same.
I've allus noticed grate success
Is mixed with troubles, more er less,
And it's the man who does the best
That gits more kicks than all the rest.

WHEN AGE COMES ON

WHEN Age comes on!—
   The deepening dusk is where the dawn
  Once glittered splendid, and the dew,
In honey-drips from red rose-lips,
  Was kissed away by me and you.—
And now across the frosty lawn
Black footprints trail, and Age comes on—
      And Age comes on!
  And biting wild-winds whistle through
Our tattered hopes—and Age comes on!

     When Age comes on!—
O tide of raptures, long withdrawn,
  Flow back in summer floods, and fling
Here at our feet our childhood sweet,
  And all the songs we used to sing! . . .
Old loves, old friends—all dead and gone—
Our old faith lost—and Age comes on—
      And Age comes on!
  Poor hearts! have we not anything
But longings left when Age comes on?

THE CIRCUS-DAY PARADE

OH! the Circus-Day Parade! How the bugles
    played and played!
And how the glossy horses tossed their flossy manes
    and neighed,
As the rattle and the rhyme of the tenor-drummer's
    time
Filled all the hungry hearts of us with melody sub-
    lime!

How the grand band-wagon shone with a splendor
    all its own,
And glittered with a glory that our dreams had
    never known!
And how the boys behind, high and low of every
    kind,
Marched in unconscious capture, with a rapture un-
    defined!

How the horsemen, two and two, with their plumes
    of white and blue
And crimson, gold and purple, nodding by at me
    and you,

Waved the banners that they bore, as the knights in
    days of yore,
Till our glad eyes gleamed and glistened like the
    spangles that they wore!

How the graceless-graceful stride of the elephant
    was eyed,
And the capers of the little horse that cantered at
    his side!
How the shambling camels, tame to the plaudits of
    their fame,
With listless eyes came silent, masticating as they
    came.

How the cages jolted past, with each wagon bat-
    tened fast,
And the mystery within it only hinted of at last
From the little grated square in the rear, and nos-
    ing there
The snout of some strange animal that sniffed the
    outer air!

And, last of all, The Clown, making mirth for all
    the town,
With his lips curved ever upward and his eyebrows
    ever down,
And his chief attention paid to the little mule that
    played
A tattoo on the dashboard with his heels, in the
    Parade.

Oh! the Circus-Day Parade! How the bugles
    played and played!
And how the glossy horses tossed their flossy manes
    and neighed,
As the rattle and the rhyme of the tenor-drummer's
    time
Filled all the hungry hearts of us with melody sub-
    lime!

WHEN THE FROST IS ON THE PUNKIN

WHEN the frost is on the punkin and the
    fodder's in the shock,
And you hear the kyouck and gobble of the strut-
    tin' turkey-cock,
And the clackin' of the guineys, and the cluckin' of
    the hens,
And the rooster's hallylooyer as he tiptoes on the
    fence;
O, it's then's the times a feller is a-feelin' at his
    best,
With the risin' sun to greet him from a night of
    peaceful rest,
As he leaves the house, bareheaded, and goes out
    to feed the stock,
When the frost is on the punkin and the fodder's
    in the shock.

They's something kindo' harty-like about the at-
    musfere
When the heat of summer's over and the coolin' fall
    is here—
Of course we miss the flowers, and the blossums on
    the trees,
And the mumble of the hummin'-birds and buzzin'
    of the bees;

But the air's so appetizin'; and the landscape
  through the haze
Of a crisp and sunny morning of the airly autumn
  days
Is a pictur' that no painter has the colorin' to
  mock—
When the frost is on the punkin and the fodder's in
  the shock.

The husky, rusty russel of the tossels of the corn,
And the raspin' of the tangled leaves, as golden as
  the morn;
The stubble in the furries—kindo' lonesome-like,
  but still
A-preachin' sermuns to us of the barns they growed
  to fill;
The strawstack in the medder, and the reaper in the
  shed;
The hosses in theyr stalls below—the clover over-
  head!—
O, it sets my hart a-clickin' like the tickin' of a
  clock,
When the frost is on the punkin and the fodder's
  in the shock!

Then your apples all is getherd, and the ones a
  feller keeps
Is poured around the celler-floor in red and yeller
  heaps;

And your cider-makin' 's over, and your wimmern-
    folks is through
With their mince and apple-butter, and theyr souse
    and saussage, too! . . .
I don't know how to tell it—but ef sich a thing
    could be
As the Angels wantin' boardin', and they'd call
    around on *me*—
I'd want to 'commodate 'em—all the whole-indurin'
    flock—
When the frost is on the punkin and the fodder's in
    the shock!

THAT NIGHT

YOU and I, and that night, with its perfume
    and glory!—
  The scent of the locusts—the light of the moon;
And the violin weaving the waltzers a story,
  Enmeshing their feet in the weft of the tune,
    Till their shadows uncertain
    Reeled round on the curtain,
  While under the trellis we drank in the June.

Soaked through with the midnight the cedars were
      sleeping,
  Their shadowy tresses outlined in the bright
Crystal, moon-smitten mists, where the fountain's
    heart, leaping
  Forever, forever burst, full with delight;
    And its lisp on my spirit
    Fell faint as that near it
  Whose love like a lily bloomed out in the night.

O your glove was an odorous sachet of blisses!
  The breath of your fan was a breeze from
    Cathay!
And the rose at your throat was a nest of spilled
    kisses!—
  And the music!—in fancy I hear it to-day,
    As I sit here, confessing
    Our secret, and blessing
  My rival who found us, and waltzed you away.

THE BAT

I

THOU dread, uncanny thing,
  With fuzzy breast and leathern wing,
    In mad, zigzagging flight,
  Notching the dusk, and buffeting
    The black cheeks of the night,
        With grim delight!

II

What witch's hand unhasps
    Thy keen claw-cornered wings
    From under the barn roof, and flings
  Thee forth, with chattering gasps,
        To scud the air,
  And nip the ladybug, and tear
  Her children's hearts out unaware?

III

  The glowworm's glimmer, and the bright,
  Sad pulsings of the firefly's light,
    Are banquet lights to thee.
  O less than bird, and worse than beast,
  Thou Devil's self, or brat, at least,
    Grate not thy teeth at me!

ON THE DEATH OF LITTLE MAHALA
ASHCRAFT

"LITTLE Haly! Little Haly!" cheeps the robin
  in the tree;
"Little Haly!" sighs the clover, "Little Haly!"
 moans the bee;
"Little Haly! Little Haly!" calls the killdeer at
 twilight;
And the katydids and crickets hollers "Haly!" all
 the night.

The sunflowers and the hollyhawks droops over the
 garden fence;
The old path down the garden walks still holds her
 footprints' dents;
And the well-sweep's swingin' bucket seems to wait
 fer her to come
And start it on its wortery errant down the old bee-
 gum.

The beehives all is quiet; and the little Jersey steer,
When any one comes nigh it, acts so lonesome-like
 and queer;

And the little Banty chickens kindo' cutters faint
and low,
Like the hand that now was feedin' 'em was one
they didn't know.

They's sorrow in the waivin' leaves of all the apple
trees;
And sorrow in the harvest-sheaves, and sorrow in
the breeze;
And sorrow in the twitter of the swallers 'round the
shed;
And all the song her redbird sings is "Little Haly's
dead!"

The medder 'pears to miss her, and the pathway
through the grass,
Whare the dewdrops ust to kiss her little bare feet
as she passed;
And the old pin in the gate-post seems to kindo'-
sorto' doubt
That Haly's little sunburnt hands'll ever pull it out.

Did her father er her mother ever love her more'n
me,
Er her sisters er her brother prize her love more
tendurly?
I question—and what answer?—only tears, and
tears alone,
And ev'ry neghbor's eyes is full o' tear-drops as my
own.

"Little Haly! Little Haly!" cheeps the robin in the
    tree;
"Little Haly!" sighs the clover, "Little Haly!"
    moans the bee;
"Little Haly! Little Haly!" calls the killdeer at twi-
    light,
And the katydids and crickets hollers "Haly!" all
    the night.

THE MULBERRY TREE

O, IT'S many's the scenes which is dear to my
mind
As I think of my childhood so long left behind;
The home of my birth, with its old puncheon-floor,
And the bright morning-glorys that growed round
the door;
The warped clabboard roof whare the rain it run off
Into streams of sweet dreams as I laid in the loft,
Countin' all of the joys that was dearest to me,
And a-thinkin' the most of the mulberry tree.

And to-day as I dream, with both eyes wide-awake,
I can see the old tree, and its limbs as they shake,
And the long purple berries that rained on the
ground
Whare the pastur' was bald whare we trommpt it
around.
And again, peekin' up through the thick leafy shade,
I can see the glad smiles of the friends when I
strayed
With my little bare feet from my own mother's knee
To foller them off to the mulberry tree.

Leanin' up in the forks, I can see the old rail,
And the boy climbin' up it, claw, tooth, and toe-
nail,

834

And in fancy can hear, as he spits on his hands,
The ring of his laugh and the rip of his pants.
But that rail led to glory, as certin and shore
As I'll never climb thare by that rout' any more—
What was all the green lauruls of Fame unto me,
With my brows in the boughs of the mulberry tree!

Then it's who can fergit the old mulberry tree
That he knowed in the days when his thoughts was
    as free
As the flutterin' wings of the birds that flew out
Of the tall wavin' tops as the boys come about?
O, a crowd of my memories, laughin' and gay,
Is a-climbin' the fence of that pastur' to-day,
And a-pantin' with joy, as us boys ust to be,
They go racin' acrost fer the mulberry tree.

AUGUST

O MELLOW month and merry month,
　　Let me make love to you,
And follow you around the world
　　As knights their ladies do.
I thought your sisters beautiful,
　　Both May and April, too,
But April she had rainy eyes,
　　And May had eyes of blue.

And June—I liked the singing
　　Of her lips—and liked her smile—
But all her songs were promises
　　Of something, after while;
And July's face—the lights and shades
　　That may not long beguile
With alternations o'er the wheat
　　The dreamer at the stile.

But you!—ah, you are tropical,
　　Your beauty is so rare;
Your eyes are clearer, deeper eyes
　　Than any, anywhere;
Mysterious, imperious,
　　Deliriously fair,
O listless Andalusian maid,
　　With bangles in your hair!

TO MY OLD FRIEND, WILLIAM LEACH-
MAN

FER forty year and better you have been a
    friend to me,
Through days of sore afflictions and dire adversity,
You allus had a kind word of counsul to impart,
Which was like a healin' 'intment to the sorrow of
    my hart.

When I buried my first womern, William Leach-
    man, it was you
Had the only consolation that I could listen to—
Fer I knowed you had gone through it and had
    rallied from the blow,
And when you said I'd do the same, I knowed you'd
    ort to know.

But that time I'll long remember; how I wundered
    here and thare—
Through the settin'-room and kitchen, and out in
    the open air—
And the snowflakes whirlin', whirlin', and the fields
    a frozen glare,
And the neghbors' sleds and wagons congergatin'
    ev'rywhare.

I turned my eyes to'rds heaven, but the sun was hid
   away;
I turned my eyes to'rds earth again, but all was cold
   and gray;
And the clock, like ice a-crackin', clickt the icy
   hours in two—
And my eyes'd never thawed out ef it hadn't been
   fer you!

We set thare by the smoke-house—me and you out
   thare alone—
Me a-thinkin'—you a-talkin' in a soothin' under-
   tone—
You a-talkin'—me a-thinkin' of the summers long
   ago,
And a-writin' "Marthy—Marthy" with my finger in
   the snow!

William Leachman, I can see you jest as plane as
   I could then;
And your hand is on my shoulder, and you rouse
   me up again;
And I see the tears a-drippin' from your own eyes,
   as you say:
"Be rickonciled and bear it—we but linger fer a
   day!"

At the last Old Settlers' Meetin' we went j'intly,
   you and me—
Your hosses and my wagon, as you wanted it to be;

And sence I can remember, from the time we've
    neghbored here,
In all sich friendly actions you have double-done
    your sheer.

It was better than the meetin', too, that nine-mile
    talk we had
Of the times when we first settled here and travel
    was so bad;
When we had to go on hoss-back, and sometimes on
    "Shanks's mare,"
And "blaze" a road fer them behind that had to
    travel thare.

And now we was a-trottin' 'long a level gravel pike,
In a big two-hoss road-wagon, jest as easy as you
    like—
Two of us on the front seat, and our wimmern-folks
    behind,
A-settin' in theyr Winsor-cheers in perfect peace of
    mind!

And we pinted out old landmarks, nearly faded out
    of sight:—
Thare they ust to rob the stage-coach; thare Gash
    Morgan had the fight
With the old stag-deer that pronged him—how he
    battled fer his life,
And lived to prove the story by the handle of his
    knife.

Thare the first griss-mill was put up in the Settle-
ment, and we
Had tuck our grindin' to it in the Fall of Forty-
three—
When we tuck our rifles with us, techin' elbows all
the way,
And a-stickin' right together ev'ry minute, night
and day.

Thare ust to stand the tavern that they called the
"Travelers' Rest,"
And thare, beyent the covered bridge, "The Coun-
terfitters' Nest"—
Whare they claimed the house was ha'nted—that a
man was murdered thare,
And burried underneath the floor, er 'round the
place somewhare.

And the old Plank-road they laid along in Fifty-one
er two—
You know we talked about the times when the old
road was new:
How "Uncle Sam" put down that road and never
taxed the State
Was a problum, don't you rickollect, we couldn't
*dim*onstrate?

Ways was devius, William Leachman, that me and
you has past;
But as I found you true at first, I find you true at
last;

And, now the time's a-comin' mighty nigh our jur-
    ney's end,
I want to throw wide open all my soul to you, my
    friend.

With the stren'th of all my bein', and the heat of
    hart and brane,
And ev'ry livin' drop of blood in artery and vane,
I love you and respect you, and I venerate your
    name,
Fer the name of William Leachman and True Man-
    hood's jest the same!

THE GUIDE
IMITATED

WE rode across the level plain—
  We—my sagacious guide and I.—
He knew the earth—the air—the sky;
He knew when it would blow or rain,
And when the weather would be dry:
The bended blades of grass spake out
To him when Redskins were about;
The wagon tracks would tell him too,
The very day that they rolled through:
He knew their burden—whence they came—
If any horse along were lame,
And what its owner ought to do;
He knew when it would snow; he knew,
By some strange intuition, when
The buffalo would overflow
The prairies like a flood, and then
Recede in their stampede again.
He knew all things—yea, he did know
The brand of liquor in my flask,
And many times did tilt it up,
Nor halt or hesitate one whit,
Nor pause to slip the silver cup
From off its crystal base, nor ask

Why I preferred to drink from it.
And more and more I plied him, and
Did query of him o'er and o'er,
And seek to lure from him the lore
By which the man did understand
These hidden things of sky and land:
And, wrought upon, he sudden drew
His bridle—wheeled, and caught my hand—
Pressed it, as one that loved me true,
And bade me listen.
. . . . There be few
Like tales as strange to listen to!
He told me all—How, when a child,
The Indians stole him—there he laughed—
"They stole me and I stole their craft!"
Then slowly winked both eyes, and smiled,
And went on ramblingly,—"And they—
They reared me, and I ran away—
'Twas winter, and the weather wild;
And, caught up in the awful snows
That bury wilderness and plain,
I struggled on until I froze
My feet ere human hands again
Were reached to me in my distress,—
And lo, since then not any rain
May fall upon me anywhere,
Nor any cyclone's cussedness
Slip up behind me unaware,—
Nor any change of cold, or heat,
Or blow, or snow, but I do know
It's coming, days and days before;—

I know it by my frozen feet—
I know it by my itching heels,
And by the agony one feels
Who knows that scratching nevermore
Will bring to him the old and sweet
Relief he knew ere thus endowed
With knowledge that a certain cloud
Will burst with storm on such a day,
And when a snow will fall, and—nay,
I speak not falsely when I say
That by my tingling heels and toes
I measure time, and can disclose
The date of month—the week—and lo,
The very day and minute—yea—
Look at your watch!—An hour ago
And twenty minutes I did say
Unto myself with bitter laugh,
'In less than one hour and a half
Will I be drunken!' Is it so?"

SUTTER'S CLAIM

SAY! *you* feller! *You*—
    With that spade and the pick!—
What do you 'pose to do
    On this side o' the crick?
Goin' to tackle this claim? Well, I reckon
    You'll let up ag'in, purty quick!

No bluff, understand,—
    But the same has been tried,
And the claim never panned—
    Or the fellers has lied,—
For they tell of a dozen that tried it,
    And quit it most onsatisfied.

The luck's dead ag'in' it!—
    The first man I see
That stuck a pick in it
    Proved *that* thing to me,—
For he sort o' took down, and got homesick,
    And went back whar he'd orto be!

Then others they worked it
    Some—more or less,

But finally shirked it,
　In grades of distress,—
With an eye out—a jaw or skull busted,
　Or some sort o' seriousness.

The *last* one was plucky—
　He wasn't afeerd,
And bragged he was "lucky,"
　And said that "he'd heerd
A heap of bluff-talk," and swore awkard
　He'd work any claim that he keered!

Don't you strike nary lick
　With that pick till I'm through;
This-here feller talked slick
　And as peart-like as you!
And he says: "I'll abide here
　As long as I please!"

But he didn't. . . . He died here—
　And I'm his disease!

DOLORES

LITHE-ARMED, and with satin-soft shoulders
   As white as the cream-crested wave;
With a gaze dazing every beholder's,
   She holds every gazer a slave:
Her hair, a fair haze, is outfloated
   And flared in the air like a flame;
Bare-breasted, bare-browed and bare-throated—
   Too smooth for the soothliest name.

She wiles you with wine, and wrings for you
   Ripe juices of citron and grape;
She lifts up her lute and sings for you
   Till the soul of you seeks no escape;
And you revel and reel with mad laughter,
   And fall at her feet, at her beck,
And the scar of her sandal thereafter
   You wear like a gyve round your neck.

MY FIDDLE

MY fiddle?—Well, I kindo' keep her handy,
    don't you know!
Though I ain't so much inclined to tromp the strings
    and switch the bow
As I was before the timber of my elbows got so dry,
And my fingers was more limber-like and caperish
    and spry;
        Yit I can plonk and plunk and plink,
          And tune her up and play,
        And jest lean back and laugh and wink
          At ev'ry rainy day!

My playin' 's only middlin'—tunes I picked up when
    a boy—
The kindo'-sorto' fiddlin' that the folks call "cor-
    daroy";
"The Old Fat Gal," and "Rye-straw," and "My
  Sailyor's on the Sea,"
Is the old cowtillions *I* "saw" when the ch'ice is
    left to me;
        And so I plunk and plonk and plink,
          And rosum-up my bow
        And play the tunes that makes you think
          The devil's in your toe!

I was allus a-romancin', do-less boy, to tell the
    truth,
A-fiddlin' and a-dancin', and a-wastin' of my youth,
And a-actin' and a-cuttin'-up all sorts o' silly pranks
That wasn't worth a button of anybody's thanks!
        But they tell me, when I used to plink
          And plonk and plunk and play,
        My music seemed to have the kink
          O' drivin' cares away!

That's how this here old fiddle's won my hart's
    indurin' love!
From the strings acrost her middle, to the
    schreechin' keys above—
From her "apern," over "bridge," and to the ribbon
    round her throat,
She's a wooin', cooin' pigeon, singin' "Love me"
    ev'ry note!
        And so I pat her neck, and plink
          Her strings with lovin' hands,—
        And, list'nin' clos't, I sometimes think
          She kindo' understands!

NORTH AND SOUTH

OF the North I wove a dream,
　All bespangled with the gleam
　Of the glancing wings of swallows
Dipping ripples in a stream,
That, like a tide of wine,
Wound through lands of shade and shine
Where purple grapes hung bursting on the
　　　vine.

And where orchard-boughs were bent
Till their tawny fruitage blent
　With the golden wake that marked the
Way the happy reapers went;
Where the dawn died into noon
As the May-mists into June,
And the dusk fell like a sweet face in a
　　　swoon.

Of the South I dreamed: And there
Came a vision clear and fair
　As the marvelous enchantments
Of the mirage of the air;

And I saw the bayou-trees,
With their lavish draperies,
Hang heavy o'er the moon-washed cypress-
      knees.

Peering from lush fens of rice,
I beheld the Negro's eyes,
   Lit with that old superstition
Death itself can not disguise;
And I saw the palm-tree nod
Like an Oriental god,
And the cotton froth and bubble from the
      pod.

And I dreamed that North and South,
With a sigh of dew and drouth,
   Blew each unto the other
The salute of lip and mouth;
And I wakened, awed and thrilled—
Every doubting murmur stilled
In the silence of the dream I found fulfilled.

THE DAYS GONE BY

O THE days gone by! O the days gone by!
The apples in the orchard, and the pathway
      through the rye;
The chirrup of the robin, and the whistle of the
      quail
As he piped across the meadows sweet as any night-
      ingale;
When the bloom was on the clover, and the blue
      was in the sky,
And my happy heart brimmed over, in the days
      gone by.

In the days gone by, when my naked feet were
      tripped
By the honeysuckle tangles where the water-lilies
      dipped,
And the ripples of the river lipped the moss along
      the brink
Where the placid-eyed and lazy-footed cattle came
      to drink,
And the tilting snipe stood fearless of the truant's
      wayward cry
And the splashing of the swimmer, in the days gone
      by.

O the days gone by! O the days gone by!
The music of the laughing lip, the luster of the eye;
The childish faith in fairies, and Aladdin's magic
    ring—
The simple, soul-reposing, glad belief in every
    thing,—
When life was like a story holding neither sob nor
    sigh,
In the golden olden glory of the days gone by.

THE CLOVER

SOME sings of the lilly, and daisy, and rose,
  And the pansies and pinks that the Summer-
    time throws
In the green grassy lap of the medder that lays
Blinkin' up at the skyes through the sunshiny days;
But what is the lilly and all of the rest
Of the flowers, to a man with a hart in his brest
That was dipped brimmin' full of the honey and
    dew
Of the sweet clover-blossoms his babyhood knew?

I never set eyes on a clover-field now,
Er fool round a stable, er climb in the mow,
But my childhood comes back jest as clear and as
    plane
As the smell of the clover I'm sniffin' again;
And I wunder away in a barefooted dream,
Whare I tangle my toes in the blossoms that gleam
With the dew of the dawn of the morning of love
Ere it wept ore the graves that I'm weepin' above.

854

And so I love clover—it seems like a part
Of the sacerdest sorrows and joys of my hart;
And wharever it blossoms, oh, thare let me bow
And thank the good God as I'm thankin' Him now;
And I pray to Him still fer the stren'th when I die,
To go out in the clover and tell it good-by,
And lovin'ly nestle my face in its bloom
While my soul slips away on a breth of purfume.

GEORGE A. CARR

O PLAYMATE of the far-away
 And dear delights of Boyhood's day,
And friend and comrade true and tried
Through length of years of life beside,
I bid you thus a fond farewell
Too deep for words or tears to tell.

But though I lose you, nevermore
To greet you at the open door,
To grasp your hand or see your smile,
I shall be thankful all the while
Because your love and loyalty
Have made a happier world for me.

So rest you, Playmate, in that land
Still hidden from us by His hand,
Where you may know again in truth
All of the glad days of your youth—
As when in days of endless ease
We played beneath the apple trees.